My Shepherd:

The 23rd Psalm Through the Eyes of a Lost & Found Sheep

Rose Schmidt

Cover photo and bookmark page photos courtesy of Emily Ruckert, as well as all others indicated by her name in book.

This book is available online from www.amazon.com
It's also available as an eBook on Kindle.

Dedication

This book is dedicated to our whole extended family, but especially:

To my dearly beloved husband, Dave Schmidt, who's been so incredible, loving me as I am, making me laugh, and picking up the slack while I was on a writing rampage.

To our beloved children who've been such encouragers, prodding me on: Dan, Tom, and Steve Savitsky, Sarah Escobar, Ben and Luke Schmidt; and their very loved spouses and our grandchildren (some yet to come even, perhaps).

Blessed be my Lord, "the author and perfecter of faith![1]

---

[1] Hebrews 12:2

Here are two translations of the 23rd Psalm for reference. I'll be using the New American Standard Bible (NASB) throughout unless otherwise indicated.

Psalm 23

"The Lord is my shepherd,
I shall not want.
He makes me lie down in green pastures;
He leads me beside quiet waters.
He restores my soul;
He guides me in the paths of righteousness
For His name's sake.
Even though I walk through
the valley of the shadow of
death, I fear no evil,
for You are with me; Your rod and Your staff, they comfort me.
You prepare a table before me in the presence of my enemies; You have anointed my head with oil; My cup overflows.
Surely goodness and lovingkindness will follow me all the days of my life, and I will dwell in the house of the Lord forever."

New American Standard Bible (NASB)

Psalm 23

"The Lord is my shepherd;
I shall not want.
He maketh me to lie down in green pastures;
He leadeth me beside the still waters.
He restoreth my soul.
He leadeth me in paths of righteousness for His name's sake.
Yea, though I walk through the valley of the shadow of death, I will fear no evil, for Thou art with me;
Thy rod and Thy staff, they comfort me.
Thou preparest a table before me in the presence of mine enemies; Thou anointest my head with oil; my cup runneth over.
Surely goodness and mercy shall follow me all the days of my life, and I will dwell in the house of the Lord forever."

The Authorized (King James) Version (KJV)

Table of Contents

The Connection

The 23rd Psalm, sometimes just called the shepherd psalm, is familiar to many of us. We've often heard it at hard times in our lives, like at a funeral, when we're grieving over a loved one. It's been an incredible comfort to me in those times, yes, but it's not just for the end of life. This beautiful psalm oozes hope and restoration, courage and contentment — for right now!

But before we start may I share with you a little personal background?

My journey toward my Shepherd started 44 years ago, and He's been faithful and good through every twist and turn, every heartbreak.

The first time I felt a true connection with the 23rd Psalm was the summer of 1976. Sitting in the Dallas-Fort Worth International Airport by myself in the wee hours of the morning, I was scared to death. After a red-eye flight that took me from Maryland to Dallas, I had to wait several hours until a van from the Bible college would arrive to take me to campus. For many 20-year-old girls, flying halfway across the country alone is nothing, par for the course. But I was sickeningly shy and hadn't ventured far from home much, just commuting to a local college from the safe little cocoon of my parents' home. Somehow, though, the Lord had infused me with *just enough* courage to get me through the flight to Dallas. So I sat there at a little table in the airport, pretty much immovable, surrounded by enough luggage to last four times the time I'd be on campus. That worked fairly well until I realized I absolutely had to go to the bathroom. But the problem was I'd barely been able to drag my ridiculously excessive baggage that far and didn't see how I could get it to the bathroom, let alone tend to it from under the stall. There were no wheels on the average person's luggage in those days and the luggage probably weighed a great deal more than I did. That meant I had to ask for help, which was way out of character for me.

Back then flying was different, minus all the security precautions we have today. There were no warnings blasted through the air about not touching packages or luggage or anything else left behind, with the unspoken suggestion it could and might contain a bomb. So I spotted a middle-aged lady sitting near me in the waiting area, and my desperation overshadowed my cowardice. I asked her to watch my luggage while I ran to the restroom. With a warmth of compassion, she readily agreed. Her simple, unexpected kindness marked the very first time on that trip I really felt the Lord's presence, His tender care for me. The 23rd Psalm, which I'd read in the few, short months between giving my life to the Lord and hopping on that plane, came to life for me right then and there. Starting with that comforting interaction, and all the way through that summer, that psalm was like a lifeline and a warm, fuzzy blanket. It became my connection to the Lord who was tenderly shepherding me every step of the way on that trip.

A second before I'd swallowed my pride and asked for help, I'd viewed many of the people in that airport with apprehension, fear even, almost as if they were my enemies. And that's how I'd begun seeing strangers, particularly since I'd had a harrowing encounter the year before.

At 19 and naive, I'd foolishly gotten on a motorcycle with a guy I'd just met at a club who offered me a ride to "the party." (My friend's party, I stupidly presumed.) But as it turned out, it wasn't my friend's party that he took me to at all, but a different kind of party altogether; and I had my first encounter with a real biker gang. While two of the guys were occupied discussing what they had in mind to do with me, I somehow slipped away and ran for my life. Petrified, and without a clue where I was going, I kept running until I finally hit familiar territory. Just as I was about to dash across the on-ramp to the beltway, a safe-looking (nerdy, some would say) stranger about to get on the Washington Beltway offered me a ride. You'd think I would have learned my lesson; but there were no cell phones back then, and I was *desperate* to get away from the bikers. I got in. Well, the second guy who was supposed to be rescuing me turned out to be much worse than the bikers. I'm telling you this convoluted story that I'm not proud of to paint for you the picture of the *very lost* sheep I had been just about a year before the airport scene. God's merciful hand protected me even when my own foolishness put me in that awful situation. By God's grace I escaped, miraculously unscathed, but it was a very close call. So close that by the time I arrived at my friend's house I was literally trembling uncontrollably. Have you ever seen anyone truly tremble? I hadn't, and I hope I never do again. But the Lord had already started wooing me, teaching me to trust Him, even back then. Little by little, He was drawing me to Himself and to the Bible, His love letter to us.

So by the time I was at the airport that next year, I was filled with a combination of gratefulness to my God who'd recently snatched me out of the fire and called me His child, completely rearranging my life, and a pretty big dose of fear of strangers. My conversion was so genuine though that when I'd felt the Lord calling me to leave behind my friends, my sinful way of life, my family (even a nephew I loved dearly who was hospitalized with spinal meningitis), I went and didn't look back. But at first it was with trepidation.

Very early on as a new Christian I memorized the 23rd Psalm, and the Lord used it right then and there. Sitting at that airport table He showed me He was with me as He prepared "a table before me in the presence of my enemies." (Psalm 23, verse 5) All the soothing words of that psalm rolled over my spirit to comfort me and prod me on with the complete assurance that my Lord cared for me, his little lost sheep that He'd found wandering. That was just the beginning. Over the course of that summer, it seemed like every verse of the 23rd Psalm was illuminated in my life.

Verse by verse, in the next six chapters, let's pull apart the 23rd Psalm together, okay?

Introduction

"... He said to him, 'Go home to your people and report to them what great things the Lord has done for you, and how He had mercy on you.' " (Mark 5:19)

Those instructions from Jesus, (though in a totally different context) reflect the motivation behind mingling my own story with our look at the 23rd Psalm. Because, my dear ones, you're my people, my family. I'm writing this book for you because I love you dearly. And in case a total stranger, or a friend, someday gets ahold of a copy, I'll tell you straight out in advance, I love you too. (When I fell in love with Jesus, I fell in love with His children, and that makes you "my peeps.") So for it to be personal for you, it has to be personal for me. And the only way I know to do that is to intertwine my story of the great and merciful things the Lord has done for me with David's shepherd psalm.

And why the title? Why would we be looking at the 23rd Psalm through the eyes of a "Lost and Found Sheep"?

Isn't the "lost and found" just a bin somewhere that's overflowing with useless discards until someone finally tosses them or gives them to charity? (Unless, of course, they're ours!) But here we're looking at sheep: valued even when they were lost, then claimed and redeemed and cared for by the Chief Shepherd. My Shepherd! And, if not now, hopefully someday soon, yours.

I'm praying you too will come away calling Him, intimately, "*my* Shepherd," as David did in the very first line of this beloved psalm. Not just any old shepherd, but *your* Shepherd. Wherever we are on that journey, let's let God open our eyes to who He is and to some of the more subtle things He's doing even now in our lives.

1. "The Lord is my shepherd, I shall not want." (Psalm 23: 1)

Well, we pretty much have to break this verse down piece by piece if we're going to begin with a firm foundation.

A. "The Lord is my shepherd…"[2]

Is He, and what does it mean?

Before we even get to the shepherd part, He's got to be Lord. Your Lord. Even if you're pretty well convinced He is, let's look a little deeper. And if you're even slightly unsure, it's all the more critical.

1. Lord?

"Lord" is a term most Christians are so familiar with they could almost trip over it without taking notice. But do we understand it? Basically, the lower-cased version of the word (lord) refers to a flesh and blood human being having power and authority over us, not an equal. In the U.K. it designates a man of high rank or office; a master or ruler, someone you'd defer to

[2] Psalm 23:1

unless you were of equal or higher rank. When we use the capitalized version, Lord, we're describing God Himself. He is the only being who has ALL power and authority. When we acknowledge that He is Lord, we are placing Him in the position He deserves and ourselves in a place of submission. He is worthy of our reverence, honor, and respect. It is essential that we get this part right: He is God, and we are not!

The word we know as "Lord" is sometimes rendered Yahweh or Yhwh (Hebrew), Kyrios/Kurios (Greek), or Adonai (Hebrew), each used in a distinct, personal way to refer to God. But for our purposes, let's keep it simple.

You don't need to get very far in your Bible to see the eternal God, the Creator of the universe, referred to as, "the Lord God." But it's important to note the term isn't introduced until the second chapter, *after* the relationship between God and man, Creator and created, is established. (God can be God, with or without us. But He can't be Lord God without someone in a relationship with Him any more than you can be a parent if you don't have any children, right?) Toward the end of the first chapter of Genesis, we read about God creating mankind: "God created man in His own image, in the image of God He created him; male and female He created them." (Genesis 1:27) This relationship of Creator to His human creation is paramount to our understanding of His position of authority. A lot of us, myself included at one time, have become accustomed to being in control, calling the shots, being independent, even rebellious. I definitely was. So the notion of God having authority may take some of you a while to get used to. But it's actually freeing.

So now we see in the next chapter for the very first time God referred to as, "Lord God." (Genesis 2:4) The phrase now makes sense in the context of our relationship as His created children to Him, our Heavenly Father and Creator. Thus the title, "Lord God," is rightly bestowed upon Him. Our God chose to bring us into existence; we were not an accident. And He desires, as we'll see in subsequent verses, to be in a deep, abiding relationship with us.

The basic sense of the word "lord" is given in my handy, old Webster's dictionary[3] as, "loaf keeper," or "one who feeds dependents." Do we see ourselves as dependent on Him? He created us, He lovingly feeds us, He constantly cares for us.

And if that wasn't enough, He sent His Son Jesus Christ, God incarnate (God taking on human flesh), to die for us. How much more could we require to acknowledge Him as Lord? That's who He is, whether we recognize Him or we refuse to.

"Being found in appearance as a man, He humbled Himself by becoming obedient to the point of death, even death on a cross. For this reason also, God highly exalted Him, and bestowed on Him the name which is above every name, so that at the name of Jesus EVERY KNEE WILL BOW, of those who are in heaven and on earth and under the earth, and that every tongue will confess that Jesus Christ is Lord, to the glory of God the Father." (Philippians 2:8-11)

So why wait? If you've never from your deepest being called the God who made you, "Lord," and meant it, I plead with you, stop and give it some thought.

The apostle Thomas referred to Him as, "My Lord and my God!" (John 20:28) But Thomas is only recorded as uttering that declaration *after* he went through a period of unbelief and doubt. If you are still struggling, keep going, and get to know Him; but don't delay. Those who seek Him, truly do find Him.[4] I did, and I didn't even know I was looking. Jesus really is my Lord and my God. On His terms, not mine. Which requires humility, a lot of it.

---

[3] *Webster's New World College Dictionary,* Fourth Edition, Michael Agnes, Ed. (New York, New York: Macmillan USA, 1999), Pg. 848.

[4] Jeremiah 29:11-13

2. Shepherd

Now let's look at the second part of this verse, "The Lord is my shepherd."[5] *My* shepherd? Yours?

What does it look like for the Lord to be your shepherd? What does this metaphor mean? To really appreciate this image, we first must have some idea what the job of a shepherd is, and what kind of shepherd the Lord is. And then we'd have to see ourselves as sheep. Right? So let's start with the shepherd.

David, who wrote the 23rd Psalm, was a shepherd. He was also the second king of Israel. Does it seem unusual to you for a simple shepherd to be selected by God to be king over His people? Someone who took care of dirty sheep? God may have seen this ability to shepherd well as an important qualification, and an important image for us to tuck away with much more far-reaching fulfillment.

The first time we hear of David, he is out "tending the sheep." (1st Samuel 16:11). When, just before that, the prophet Samuel came to Bethlehem and invited David's father Jesse and his sons to attend a sacrifice with him, Jesse never even bothered to bring David. He was his youngest son, maybe considered too young for such an important event. He was also needed to safeguard the sheep. David's role as shepherd (and king) can be seen as foreshadowing Jesus' roles, so let's jump ahead and look at some of the references to Jesus as shepherd.

Jesus told a parable to help His followers, including us, comprehend the role He wants to play in our lives as the "good shepherd." The entire Bible is rife with beautiful and important images of shepherds and shepherding, but this parable is

---

[5] Psalm 23:1

essential to our understanding of who Jesus is and what He came to do. It's long, but it's pretty much the key to understanding the fulfillment of the 23rd Psalm. Will you read it through? Then we can pick it apart:

" 'Truly, truly, I say to you, he who does not enter by the door into the fold of the sheep, but climbs up some other way, he is a thief and a robber. But he who enters by the door is a shepherd of the sheep. To him the doorkeeper opens, and the sheep hear his voice, and he calls his own sheep by name and leads them out. When he puts forth all his own, he goes ahead of them, and the sheep follow him because they know his voice. A stranger they simply will not follow, but will flee from him, because they do not know the voice of strangers.' This figure of speech Jesus spoke to them, but they did not understand what those things were which He had been saying to them. So Jesus said to them again, 'Truly, truly, I say to you, I am the door of the sheep. All who came before Me are thieves and robbers, but the sheep did not hear them. I am the door; if anyone enters through Me, he will be saved, and will go in and out and find pasture. The thief comes only to steal and kill and destroy; I came that they may have life, and have it abundantly. I am the good shepherd; the good shepherd lays down His life for the sheep. He who is a hired hand, and not a shepherd, who is not the owner of the sheep, sees the wolf coming, and leaves the sheep and flees, and the wolf snatches them and scatters them. He flees because he is a hired hand and is not concerned about the sheep. I am the good shepherd, and I know My own and My own know Me, even as the Father knows Me and I know the Father; and I lay down My life for the sheep. I have other sheep, which are not of this fold; I must bring them also, and they will hear My voice; and they will become one flock with one shepherd. For this reason the Father loves Me, because I lay down My life so that I may take it again. No one has taken it away from Me, but I lay it down on my own initiative. I have authority to lay it down, and I have authority to take it up again. This commandment I received from My Father.' " (John 10:1-18)

The shepherd in the 23rd Psalm points ahead to Jesus. The shepherd-Lord whom David describes depicts prophetically no one other than God incarnate, Jesus Christ. So let's dissect it a bit to see what kind of shepherd is described.

This narrative is set up like a historical battle with the forces of evil coming against the forces for good. On one side, we have a thief and a robber who creeps by insidiously, not through the door, but instead slithering in so he can't be seen. On the other side, we have the good shepherd who comes right in through the legitimate door for all to see. The doorkeeper opens to him.

When it's time for the sheep to leave the fold, their own shepherd calls them by name, opens the door, and leads them out. He goes ahead of them, protectively. His sheep follow him because they know him. They've spent enough time with him to know his voice. Think about how many people in your life you know intimately enough to recognize their voices.

The stranger, on the other hand, doesn't know the sheep. They're not his, and he's not invested in them. They don't recognize his voice, so they take off running. Smart sheep!

Who are these strangers? From verses that come before this section,[6] we can see Jesus was addressing some of the Pharisees, the religious leaders of his time who knew the Scriptures, yet they were either spiritually blind or maybe too prideful to recognize their own Messiah, Jesus (rendered "Yeshua" in Hebrew). They were not caring well for the "sheep" they had charge over. Not all Pharisees and prominent Jewish leaders rejected Jesus (Nicodemus[7] the Pharisee, who came to Jesus by night, for example, was a follower of Jesus, as was Joseph of Arimathea[8] who buried Jesus in his own tomb). But

---

[6] John 9:39-41

[7] John 3:1, 4, 9; and 7:50 and 19:39

[8] Matthew 27:57-60 and Mark 16:43

Jesus was warning His followers not to follow false shepherds, false prophets.

So Jesus, for the benefit of his hearers, states emphatically, "I am the door of the sheep. All who came before Me are thieves and robbers [e.g., false shepherds, or even false messiahs?], but the sheep did not hear them. I am the door; if anyone enters through Me, he will be saved, and will go in and out and find pasture."[9] What does He mean?

The "door" metaphor isn't really as hard to comprehend when we go to Jesus' own words to His disciples:

"Jesus said to him [Thomas], 'I am the way, and the truth, and the life; no one comes to the Father but through Me.' " (John 14:6)

Those words were clear enough to get Him crucified not much later. Jesus doesn't just declare Himself "a way," one of many alternate paths. He declares Himself the way (e.g., the only way) to the Father. And He is.

My sister, Kathy, told me she met a guy at her car dealership once. He'd had a Jewish girlfriend who'd accepted Jesus, then died. He said he was fine with God; his problem was Jesus. Kathy told him, "Jesus said, 'I am the way, and the truth, and the life; no one comes to the Father but through Me.' "[10] She continued, "Jesus is the door, and without Him we won't get in." Some might accuse her of being narrow minded with that statement, but Jesus addressed that too: "Strive to enter through the narrow door; for many, I tell you, will seek to enter and will not be able."[11]

---

[9] John 10:7(b)-9

[10] John 14:6

[11] Luke 13:24

What keeps them out? The choices they make. My sister Jeanie told me that every mistake in her life she ever made was brought about by thinking she knew better than God. She knew what she'd been taught, and in her gut knew what the right thing to do was. But she rationalized that her circumstances were somehow different and God couldn't possibly mean for her to follow such a rigid interpretation. Thinking we know what's best for ourselves more than God does changes the position we talked about earlier, by placing ourselves on the throne of our lives instead of the Lord. What else plays a part? Trying to please others? Being afraid to stand up to peer pressure because we don't want to look foolish? The wrong choices we make often bring temporary pleasure. Sin can look very enticing. But, is it worth it? Jesus cared enough to warn, "Enter through the narrow gate; for the gate is wide and the way is broad that leads to destruction, and there are many who enter through it. For the gate is small and the way is narrow that leads to life, and there are few who find it." (Matthew 7:13) The choice is yours.

In the last part of the good shepherd narrative, John 10:10-18, Jesus starts by comparing the thief with the good shepherd. Here's the difference: The thief's hidden agenda is thievery, murder, and destruction. Who does that sound like? The good shepherd, however, says He came that we might "have life, and have it abundantly,"[12] and that He "lays down His life for the sheep."[13] He did it willingly, not under compulsion, but out of love. Who does that sound like? Jesus doesn't actually leave us guessing by this point, but pointedly identifies Himself twice saying, "I am the good shepherd."[14]

Then Jesus contrasts Himself, the good shepherd, with the hired hand. And the difference is even more marked. Our good shepherd lays down His life for His sheep. No hired hand would

---

[12] John 10:10

[13] John 10:11

[14] John 10:11 & 14

likely do that. Instead the hired hand takes off, deserting the sheep for the wolf to rip apart or scatter. Why? Because he's paid labor, not a shepherd. They're not his sheep and he doesn't care about them, certainly not enough to risk his life.

But do you actually know this incredibly good shepherd we just read about? Jesus calls Himself in that parable the good shepherd. That's a very bold statement, because Jesus Himself said in another passage, "No one is good except God alone." (Luke 18:19) Thus Jesus, by calling Himself the "good" shepherd, is clearly affirming His deity. Only God is good. Think about that.

Our good shepherd is not only the Shepherd of our souls, He's also the Lamb of God who was slain for our sins! (Isaiah 53:7; John 1:29; Revelation 12:11) In our place! The only one who could do both! Pretty awesome, huh?

(Photo courtesy of Lorraine Letcavage)

3. Sheep

The role of sheep in the 23rd Psalm is implied; but you can't see the Lord as your shepherd unless you see yourself as a sheep, can you?

David's livelihood, before he became a king, was earned by shepherding sheep. He knew sheep well. Yet, in comparing himself to God in Psalm 23, David saw himself not as a shepherd, but as a lowly sheep. How about ourselves, can we envision ourselves as sheep? Let's think a little about sheep.

My husband Dave and I live in the lush Willamette Valley in western Oregon, where there are lots of sheep found grazing in our fertile grass fields. This area is known as "the grass seed capital of the world." I'm no expert on sheep, but I feel drawn to their beauty and innocence. So I did a little research to learn more about sheep, and even consulted a modern-day shepherdess living in our community. Then I watched a documentary on shepherding and sheep, honing in on one particular aspect of sheep and their significant relationships.

Research on Sheep and Their Characteristics

Since many of you don't live in "sheep country" like I do, I thought I'd just list a few of the very basic attributes and behaviors of sheep. Sheep are:

Instinctive: Because they operate on instinct, they're not going to respond to reasoning and explanations as to why they shouldn't do a certain behavior. But establishing boundaries, repetitive training, and attaching rewards and punishments to certain behaviors does work. In *Storey's Guide to Raising Sheep* by Paula Simmons and Carol Ekarius we read, "Through 'punishments' they can quickly learn to avoid certain things, like an electric fence."[15]

Emotional: "Sheep, like other mammals, are capable of displaying a full array of emotions, from anger to happiness, to the most common emotion we humans usually see when dealing with animals: fear."[16] "As much as fear reactions can be a pain in the neck for shepherds, they must remember that those reactions are genetically programmed for survival."[17]

Dependent and useful: There's a mutually-beneficial relationship between shepherds and sheep. Sheep meet the economic needs of shepherds, and the shepherds reciprocate

---

[15] Paula Simmons and Carol Ekarius, *Storey's Guide to Raising Sheep* (North Adams, MA: Storey Communications, Inc., 2001), Page 7

[16] Ibid., Pages 8-9

[17] Ibid., Page 9

by protecting and caring for the sheep. Sheep can't shear themselves and would get pretty hot without shepherds. "They [sheep] provide economically efficient food and fiber…."[18] Humans eat lamb and mutton as food sources, with lamb currently being more popular and sought after in other cultures than here in the United States. Sheep's milk is used to make cheese. Sue Weaver, in her book, *Sheep: Small-Scale Sheep Keeping*, notes: "Many of the world's great cheeses are made from ewe's milk. These include Greek Feta, Kasseri, and Manouri;... Sicilian Pepato and Ricotta Salata; and that perpetual French favorite, genuine Roquefort cheese."[19]

Gentle and vulnerable: "Sheep know they are vulnerable to predators. They are small and scrumptious creatures who don't bite or kick to defend themselves, and they rarely use their horns in self-defense."[20]

Social / Followers: "Sheep are gregarious, meaning they crowd together for reassurance and protection. They have a strong inner compulsion to follow a leader. These traits compose their flocking instinct."[21]

Reactive/Stress-driven: "Sheep are not stupid; they are reactive. Their only means of survival is to band together for protection, then run. Frightened, stressed sheep flee blindly, pack into corners, and get wedged behind gates.[22] "Prolonged stress triggers cortisol production, and elevated cortisol levels significantly reduce immunity. Stressed sheep tend not to thrive."[23]

---

[18] Ibid., Page 1

[19] Sue Weaver, *Sheep: Small-Scale Sheep Keeping* (Mount Joy, PA: CompanionHouse Books,2017), Pages 25-26

[20] Ibid., Page 59

[21] Ibid., Page 15

[22] Ibid., Page 15

[23] Ibid., Page 19

Prone to wander: Without a good shepherd, a herd animal (such as a llama), or well-constructed fences, they're likely to go astray. "Admittedly, there are some difficulties to raising sheep: They think fences are puzzles that you've placed there for them to figure out a way out of."[24]

[24] Paula Simmons and Carol Ekarius, *Storey's Guide to Raising Sheep* (North Adams, MA: Storey Communications, Inc., 2001), Page 1

Interview with Emily

After I'd gathered my research, it was time to venture out and meet with a local shepherdess, Emily Ruckert, and her sheep.

Before I could get to know her sheep, I had to first get acquainted with Emily and observe how she relates to her sheep. Years before I actually interviewed Emily, we met at a Bible study. I told her how much I loved sheep and started asking her stupid questions. I made the huge mistake of asking her if it was true that sheep were dumb animals, as some people assumed. (Oh, don't ever ask a good shepherd who loves her sheep that!) And no, she said, they're not dumb, which was confirmed in my research. But the lovingly defensive stance she took toward her sheep was just my first indication of how much she loved her sheep. It became even clearer when I interviewed her and saw her interacting with her sheep. She's very protective of her sheep, and she's trained them well. Loving the sheep is, to me, the greatest and most crucial qualification in the job description of a good shepherd. When you love well, everything else just sort of falls into place. And after seeing Emily in action, I'd definitely call her a good shepherd.

Soon after I arrived at the pasture where Emily had her sheep grazing, I noticed the sheep were well behaved, doing exactly what they were supposed to do. However, when they saw me they totally freaked out. I was a stranger, and they didn't trust me, so they scattered. But as they watched me interacting with Emily, and after she wisely told me to hide behind a bush, they got more used to my presence. At least most of them did. There was one ewe named Pig who'd started life as what Emily called a “bummer lamb.” (She was quite large!) The ewe’s mother hadn’t been able to take care of her because of mastitis, so she missed out on the very critical period of maternal bonding. The poor sheep wasn’t normal, Emily said. She was more difficult to control than any of the others. She tried to run off when Emily was herding them into the sheep-hauler truck; but, with a little more effort, Emily was able to rein even her in.

I was kind of shocked at how closely the sheep clustered together. I thought she’d need two trailers to get all the sheep in, but instead she just kept moving them forward and they scrunched in together with no room to spare. I was at first concerned, but she assured me they were fine. I guess they are pretty well padded, but it was clear from what Emily said and from what I saw that this was standard behavior for sheep. Sheep are content flocking closely together, and they aren’t designed for independent living. That’s not their nature, and they don’t seem to like being alone. (People going through our current COVID-19 viral crisis, experiencing quarantine and forced isolation, can probably relate to sheep on that.)

Emily’s sheep showed they were good at following a leader. Sometimes it was Emily herding them along, and other times she used her trained sheep dog (as she was busy explaining things to me). And it’s to their benefit that sheep refuse to follow strangers (such as myself), because otherwise thieves could just creep in and pick them out.

From my vantage point, Emily gave up a lot to care for her sheep. She started raising the orphan lambs as a younger child, and got her own ewes when she was 12, soon becoming fully invested in caring for sheep. It pretty much has become her life. She doesn’t have the luxury of doing some of the frivolous things a young woman her age takes for granted because of her responsibilities with her sheep. She needs to be there for them. (Not that she doesn’t ever get out and have fun!) But Emily’s a strong Christian, so I’ll bet she’d be the first to point out what she's given up doesn't compare to what the Good Shepherd, Jesus, gave up for us.

In one of our drives through the countryside, my husband Dave and I encountered this lamb tangled up in a thicket of briars (see photo below):

(Photo by author)

We also found one on the road another time, and I went to the house to tell the owner. He politely thanked us, but I learned from Emily that she doesn't worry when her sheep get out. They'll come back to the flock, she said. That's where they feel safe and protected. Kind of an interesting insight. If some day one of your "flock" has strayed among the brambles like that lost sheep we found, maybe Emily's outlook will give you something to hang onto as you wait for your offspring to return to the place where there's ample food for his or her thirsty soul.

(Photo by author)

As an addendum, it's been about six months since I interviewed Emily, and I just found out Pig didn't survive the winter when Emily was ill and had to be away from the barn for six days. Her sadness for and tenderness toward that feisty and difficult ewe was touching to me.

And here's an Old Testament Scripture that prefigures Jesus and displays His own tenderness toward us sheep:

"Like a shepherd He will tend His flock, in His arm He will gather the lambs and carry them in His bosom; He will gently lead the nursing ewes." (Isaiah 40:11)

That nursing ewes reference reminds me of a picture we have in our dining room. (See photo below.)

(Photo by author)

It means a lot to me because it was given to me by my brother-in-law, Billy, who, along with his sister Lorraine, has faithfully been there for my children since their older brother passed away. It depicts Jesus holding on his lap a small lamb, a nursing ewe perhaps. That picture helped carry me through a lot of very rough times raising my kids as a single parent by pointing out Jesus' character as the Shepherd of my soul. I know we have no idea what Jesus looked like, and I only treat this picture like I would an icon, a foggy surrealistic representation of something we can't see and can't depict, not an object of worship. But the tenderness it expresses from Jesus is not just extended to the little lost and found lamb Jesus is holding. His other hand is extended gently and compassionately on the mother's head. I know it's just a piece of art and not a real picture of Jesus, but it reminds me of the compassionate Jesus we read about in Scripture who touched my life in ways only He could.

Documentary: Insights on Bummer Lambs

I got a poignant and in-depth look at bummer lambs like Pig when I viewed a documentary entitled, "Sweetgrass."[25] This movie followed a group of shepherds and ranch hands making the last summer trek across Montana's Absaroka-Beartooth Mountains to find pasture in public lands for their sheep.

The lambing scene begins dramatically, zeroing in on a dark sheep pen. In it we find a ewe, possibly a mother sheep who's just given birth, with shallow, labored breathing. There's no dialogue, so we're left wondering what happened to her, whether she survived.

Next we see the shepherd scooping up a bloody newborn lamb and coaxing another ewe to follow it into a stall to feed it.

At first this ewe retreats shyly, but eventually she goes into the pen to care for the lamb. Success! Match accomplished!

But after many lambs are finished giving birth to their young, two lambs remain that have no mothers to care for them. So the shepherds set about concocting an elaborate process to try to save the babies. Sometimes the mothers themselves don't survive to care for the lambs, and other times they reject their own offspring. With Emily's bummer lamb, it was because of the mother's painful inflammation of the udder that Pig was

---

[25] *Sweetgrass*, a film by Ilisa Barbash and Lucien Castaing-Taylor (Brooklyn, NY: The Cinema Guild, Inc., 2010), used with permission.

rejected. (Mastitis is usually caused by an infection, as I learned back in the days of nursing my own babies.)

The video gave no indication what caused each of the bummer lambs to be abandoned, but the shepherds were prepared to do whatever it took to rectify the situation.

These tough, yet tender, shepherds were relentless. The first abandoned lamb they tried to seek out a mother for they'd named "Virginia." One shepherd declared, "Virginia, we've got to find you some milk!" But his attempt to find Virginia a ewe willing to let her nurse didn't go very well. The mama already had one lamb, and she was not big on sharing her milk with the bummer. When the shepherd blocked the ewe from her own lamb and tried to get her to nurse the strange baby, she would have none of it! First she just kicked against the pen wall, but finally she defiantly laid down in the pen, making it impossible for the lamb to access the teat.

So the shepherd's next plan was to get a large, plastic syringe that resembled an oversized version of a medicine dispenser I had used for my children when they were toddlers. He hand-milked the reluctant ewe's milk into the syringe, then he used the little tube he'd inserted in it to reach the abandoned lamb's mouth. Once it was set, he used the plunger end to assist in feeding the lamb. That was a stopgap measure designed to keep the lamb alive until he could find her a mother.

His next strategy was much more complex and required help from other shepherds who were standing at the ready. After assisting another mother in giving birth to a healthy lamb, our shepherd checked the birth canal to make sure that was her only lamb. When he found it was, he immediately blocked her view so she couldn't see what he was up to. Quickly, the others brought in the two rejected lambs. He then immediately set about trying to rub the mother's blood and afterbirth from her own lamb all over the bummers so she'd identify them as her own by smell. But it just wasn't quite enough for both bummer lambs, so he handed one back to the others standing by.

When the mother licks the bummer and doesn't turn away from him, like a proud papa, her shepherd jubilantly asserts, "Okay, you just got adopted."

Then they plan an even more intricate matchmaking scheme for the last rejected lamb. "We're going to pull a switch here," says our shepherd. Another ewe had lost her baby in birthing, so they peel off the skin of her dead lamb. Then they sew it together to make a little suit to slip over the bummer and staple it together to make it hold in place. "Gonna make the mother think it's her dead lamb come to life," he says. It's hard to imagine this could fool a mother, but they have a strong sense of smell, and it apparently works. Plus, a mother devoid of her baby wants very badly for that lamb to be hers.

And why is this section on bummer lambs important to our understanding of the 23rd Psalm? Because just as the bummer lambs' lives depend on being accepted and cared for, so do ours. Our Shepherd who loves us went even farther than these human shepherds did to assure we would not perish. He stepped in and took the sins that separated us from our Father on His own back, dying in our place so that we could live eternally. He restored both: our souls, and our relationship with our Father.

In fact, God went so far as to adopt us as His very own:

"But when the fullness of the time came, God sent forth His Son, born of a woman, born under the Law, so that He might redeem those who were under the Law, that we might receive the adoption as sons. Because you are sons, God has sent forth the Spirit of His Son into our hearts, crying, 'Abba! Father!' "[26]

---

[26] Galatians 4:4-6

Have you experienced rejection? I don't know if there's anyone alive who hasn't, at least to some degree. To be rejected by a parent (or anyone else we're relying on) is so unthinkable that our God addresses those who have deceived themselves into believing, "The Lord has forsaken me, and the Lord has forgotten me."[27] This is His reply:

"Can a woman forget her nursing child and have no compassion on the son of her womb? Even these may forget, but I will not forget you. Behold, I have inscribed you on the palms of My hands…."[28]

The Lord, Our Shepherd, knew rejection firsthand. His closest friends deserted Him when He was being hauled off to face His accusers. And some of the same people who earlier that week had been waving palm branches to honor him shouted, "Crucify Him!"[29] Yet on the cross He said, "Father, forgive them; for they do not know what they are doing."[30] His forgiveness extends to each of us…

B. "…I shall not want."[31]

What about this last part of the verse? Do you take it as a promise, something we can expect? Or do you take it as a command?

Well, isn't this "shall not" language similar to what's in the famous ten commandments? And I think we'd have a hard time successfully arguing that they were suggestions. Right? It depends a lot on our emphasis how that verse is taken, so let's

---

[27] Isaiah 49:14

[28] Isaiah 49:15-16(a)

[29] Matthew 27:23

[30] Luke 23:34

[31] Psalm 23:1

look at it two ways, as a promise of provision and then as a command. Okay?

Here's the promise. God is our provider, and He supplies what we need to sustain life as long as He gives us breath on this earth. Ponder that carefully. Do you believe it? The footnotes in my Bible for this verse refer to Ezekiel 34:11-13 and Philippians 4:19. The Ezekiel verse describes how God Himself will seek for us, His sheep. He'll care for us, and deliver us, and even feed us. The Philippians reference reads, "And my God will supply all your needs according to His riches in glory in Christ Jesus."[32] How wonderful to be able to trust Him as our provider! And because He provides, we don't need to worry or want. He is sovereign, and He knows what our true needs are better than we do.

We can't try to solve the world's mysteries here, but for a second let's also look at it a different way: as a command, a serious directive, one influencing our choices.

We can choose either of two paths: first, to be content with what God provides; or, second, to want more, want it our way, even want something we don't need or that might not be good for us.

Selecting the path of contentment involves trust, believing that God knows best even when we can't see it, believing if it's something we truly need, then He'll provide it if He wants us to continue on in this world. That choice requires an eternal perspective and a willingness to accept God's will over ours.

Choosing the second path, the path that breeds discontentment, tends to draw a very fine line between wants and needs. It leans in the direction of insisting on prosperity, requiring the most profitable, the easiest and most painless

---

[32] Philippians 4:19

avenues, with no regard for the cost or toll upon our souls or upon others' lives.

But what are needs anyway? In college we had an exercise in one of my classes where we were asked to divide into groups and prioritize collectively what we would need if marooned on some forsaken island. I can remember mulling it over, trying to distinguish between what was actually needed to sustain life, and what was trivial. As Christians, we know this earth is temporary, everything in it will pass away. Unless we are still alive in the end, we are going to die. (And if you've read the last book of the Bible, you're probably hoping, like me, you aren't around for that.) It's where we spend eternity that matters, and it's that eternal perspective that gives us grace to entrust everything to our Lord.

Paul, who wrote the letter to the Philippians just cited above, also said, "Not that I speak from want, for I have learned to be content in whatever circumstances I am. I know how to get along with humble means, and I also know how to live in prosperity; in any and every circumstance I have learned the secret of being filled and going hungry, both of having abundance and of suffering need. I can do all things through Him who strengthens me." (Philippians 4:11-13).

This, to me, is a reminder to myself to trust the Shepherd of my soul and be content, to choose not to want what God doesn't want for me or to be greedy. In that sense, I take it as a command that I've chosen to lay upon myself: *I shall not want!* That doesn't have to stomp out our hopes or dreams or keep us from enjoying the things God gives, but it's a caution not to hold too tightly to the things of this world. Clearly overindulgence can turn healthy desires into something sinister. Overeating, for example (gluttony, if I really want to be honest), is something I've battled lately. Sometimes the solution is as simple as substituting something healthy like fruit for the chocolates I'm craving. I *want* to want what is good. Just food for thought.

2. "He makes me lie down in green pastures; He leads me beside quiet waters." (Ps. 23:2)

(Photo by Emily Ruckert)

This verse sure presents an inviting, pastoral scene, doesn't it? Lush, green pastures; quiet or even still waters. Can you picture yourself basking in it on a fine spring day? Or is your life more lean than green, and your journey more turbulent, like white-water rafting, than sailing over quiet waters?

Well, my world was extremely fast-paced and frenzied too at one time. But even in the midst of that, I learned that if we listen intently to God's nudges and give the Lord first place in our lives He will provide times of refreshment. Sometimes He leads us out of the mighty rushing river, but sometimes He takes us straight through it. I guess I've lived through both. Probably the most intense period of my life came when I was widowed at 38, and my kids were 4, 7, 8½ and 10. However, it was also a period of major spiritual growth. God works good out of it all for us, if we're on His team, loving Him and trying to do His will. In Paul's letter to the Romans, we read:

"And we know that God causes all things to work together for good to those who love God, to those who are called according to His purpose." (Romans 8:28)

Those words have been engraved on my heart lately.

But rest and solitude are life-giving. Our God knows how to still the seas, if that's what it takes. Our bodies, our minds, and our souls need rest and down time. Jesus demonstrated through His own life on earth that He valued solitude, especially for the purpose of prayer. If you read the four parallel gospels (Matthew, Mark, Luke, and John) you'll see Jesus pulling Himself away from the crowds and praying. (Or trying to! Often He compassionately allowed them to track Him down.)

We sometimes need those quiet times to prepare for what's coming, like the calm before a tornado. But He's with us in the storm too.

I will never forget the tornado that hit College Park and Laurel, Maryland, on September 24, 2001, when I was living in Laurel and working at the University of Maryland. I have never felt anything quite so eerie as the silence, sudden stillness, and pitch darkness that swept down on us just before the tornado hit. When it cleared enough to assess the damage, we found power lines down all around the streets surrounding our corner house, but none landed in our yard. It looked like all the houses near us sustained damage, and some of their debris came to rest in our yard; but our house was passed over.

Two sisters at the University of Maryland in College Park where I worked were killed when their car was swept up by that tornado over one of the high-rise dorms, and over 50 people were injured before the tornado fizzled out. That tornado caught us by surprise. I'd lived in the Baltimore-Washington metropolitan area all my life and had never even heard of a tornado anywhere near us. Storms of life come, when least expected, but when we rest in the Lord and pray, He prepares us and sustains us when they do hit.

Are you still feeling left out of this green pasture and quiet life? Well, I've noticed when I'm carrying more than God ever intended for me to, I'm wiped out, useless, frazzled. When my husband died and I was left to raise four little children alone, I tried to take on both roles, mother and father. The very night my husband died it should have been evident I couldn't, with four children crushed to their very souls, weeping in their beds, and only one parent to lend comfort. If I had it to do over again, I'd gather them all in my bed with me and we'd all just cry it out together until we fell asleep. But I was trying to be tough, illogically thinking I had to get them to sleep so the older ones could make it to school in the morning. It got a lot worse when the teen years hit all at once (the first three were about a year and a half apart). I felt I had to fill my husband's shoes by being a harsh disciplinarian (not that he *ever* was), when what they needed was a mother. My daughter used to accuse me (when I'd get upset) of using my "man voice," trying to sound tough like a man. Her assessment maddened me even worse!

God is our Father. I learned way too late He called me to be a mother, and to entrust them to their Heavenly Father for the things that I just wasn't designed for. I don't mean I should have foregone discipline entirely, but I was constantly policing them in their teen years, distrusting and monitoring their activities, while trying to be a super mom. I failed, because I was carrying more than God called me to carry. If you ever become a single parent, this may not make sense to you at first. *Who else is going to do it*, you might wonder. But I tried so hard to do everything myself that I didn't leave room for God to be Father, God to discipline, God to allow them to fall while the stakes were still low, not way too late when it was costly. Notice the meaning behind these words of Jesus:

"Come to Me, all who are weary and heavy-laden, and I will give you rest. Take My yoke upon you and learn from Me, for I am gentle and humble in heart, and you will find rest for your souls. For My yoke is easy and My burden is light." (Matthew 11:28-30)

That yoke described above is a wooden structure that goes around the necks of two oxen to bind them together so they're not pulling in opposite directions when they're hauling a heavy load. When I was a widow, I was carrying a heavy load, but when I needed Him most I wasn't fully yoked to the Lord. I was off on my own, thinking I had to pull the whole cart myself, often without prayer, or "after-the-fact prayer" (asking God to bless the mess I'd made).

I finally learned during my kids' teen years when it all hit the fan to lean into Jesus and reset my priorities. I started setting my alarm to go off at 5:21 a.m. every morning so I'd have time alone with my Lord, soaking in His love and His peace. What a difference that extra time of refreshment made in my life! It may not at first make sense, in the economy of things, to give God an hour (or whatever we can) of our time when we're already busy. When I started giving God the first fruits of my time, putting my time with Him first instead of giving Him leftover scraps at night before I hit the pillow, I was shocked at the results. I became more relaxed, more focused, more joyful and patient, and my trust in Him began to build. The first fruits of our time may not compute if you've never heard the expression. It's based on the first fruits of their labors that the Israelites were asked to offer to God. (Exodus 23:16)

We grow plum trees, blueberries, raspberries, and strawberries in our backyard. I've noticed toward the end of the season the fruit is often substandard, some of it even comes out deformed. But the first fruits are such a delight, especially when I'm surprised by that very first, juicy, ripe strawberry. When I'm offering the Lord my time, I want to give Him my freshest time, even if it involves sacrifice. In doing so, I stopped frantically trying to accomplish everything, and started to rely on my God to reach where I couldn't and to trust Him more.

My beloved children suffered because of my attempts at extreme self-reliance until I wore myself out. I finally learned I needed to rest in the Lord's presence and pour out my heart to Him daily. I hope my kids can forgive me.

I don't know what burdens you're trying to carry, but ask the Lord whether you're taking on more than you should. In those areas where He genuinely is calling you to shoulder a lot, He will help you carry it. He's the "Helper," as the Holy Spirit is called,[33] after all! I learned one thing the hard way: if I'm pridefully carrying too much, to impress myself or others with how tough I am, why would He step in and help?

---

[33] John 14:16-26

3. "He restores my soul; He guides me in the paths of righteousness for His name's sake." (Ps. 23:3)

It's kind of a two-step process, so let's look at each part.

A. "He restores my soul."[34]

Does your soul need restoring? I didn't actually think mine did at first. In fact, even when I offered my heart to the Lord, sincerely giving Him free rein to do whatever He wanted with me, I didn't understand the full weight or impact of my own sin. This sounds really crass, but I almost thought I was doing God a favor by saying yes to Him, instead of the other way around. But shortly after I surrendered to the Lord I had a dream that permanently changed my outlook. I don't put much stock in my dreams. Very rarely do they have any spiritual implication, and I think it's dangerous to perceive every dream as some direct link with God. But this dream was definitely used by God to open my blind eyes.

I dreamed I was inside a burning building. Yet I was actually looking at it from outside through a cross section, kind of like

---

[34]Psalm 23:3

the plastic doll houses they used to make that could open up for you to peer in. Inside with me were a bunch of my friends that I used to smoke pot with, mostly blurred faces except one particular friend. When it suddenly hit me that the building I was in was going up in flames around me, I looked around at my friends' faces. They were all just totally spaced out, unaware of what was happening. Survival instinct took over and without looking back I ran! When I woke up I was stunned at what I'd just dreamed, but almost instantly saw the symbolism, the implications! I was destined for hell, had not the Lord woken me up, rescued me, redeemed my very soul! He snatched me out of the fire.

If you're thinking, "Yeah, she probably was headed for hell, but I'm not," well, I hope with all my heart you have already sincerely put your faith in Jesus. But if you haven't yet, this "all" below is pretty all-inclusive:

"All of us like sheep have gone astray. Each of us has turned to his own way; but the Lord has caused the iniquity [sin] of us all to fall on Him." (Isaiah 53:6)

On our own, "There is none righteous, not even one."[35] Indeed, "...all have sinned and fall short of the glory of God, being justified as a gift by His grace through the redemption which is in Christ Jesus; whom God displayed publicly as a propitiation in His blood through faith." (Romans 3:23-25) But this "propitiation," what in the world is that? Here's how I picture it:

Imagine a completely innocent, spotless little lamb, willingly allowing each of us — all of humanity, for all time — to cast every one of our heavy burdens of sin straight onto his back. Again and again, over and over, we thrust them upon this sinless lamb's back while he stands as a scapegoat for us, just taking it, the way a gentle and docile lamb stands still before his

---

[35] Romans 3:10

shearers. Sheep are not designed to be load-bearing pack animals, so eventually, with no other outcome possible, the lamb is crushed beneath the weight of all our ugly sins, barely recognizable in his grief, while we stand untouched, washed clean as if we'd never sinned.

That is just my imagined rendition of it. But Jesus actually did it. He is the Lamb of God, slain for our sins.[36] When John the Baptist saw Jesus He testified, "Behold, the Lamb of God who takes away the sin of the world!" (John 1:29)

Isaiah, who is said to have begun his prophetic ministry somewhere around 740 B.C.,[37] spoke this prophecy about Jesus hundreds of years before His birth:

"Surely our griefs He Himself bore, and our sorrows He carried; yet we ourselves esteemed Him stricken, smitten of God, and afflicted. But He was pierced through for our transgressions, He was crushed for our iniquities; the chastening for our well-being fell upon Him, and by His scourging we are healed. All of us like sheep have gone astray, each of us has turned to his own way; but the Lord has caused the iniquity of us all to fall on Him. He was oppressed and He was afflicted, yet He did not open His mouth; like a lamb that is led to slaughter, and like a sheep that is silent before its shearers, so He did not open His mouth.... But the Lord was pleased to crush Him, putting Him to grief; if He would render Himself as a guilt offering.... As a result of the anguish of His soul, He will see it and be satisfied; by His knowledge the Righteous One, My Servant, will justify the many, as He will bear their iniquities." (Isaiah 53:4-7, 10(a), 11)

---

[36] Revelation 5:12

[37] *The ESV Study Bible, English Standard Version* (ESV) (Wheaton, Illinois: Crossway, a publishing ministry of Good News Publishers, 2007) Pg.1233

Our pastor gave a much more theological explanation of the propitiation I attempted to portray in my simple way. But eventually he summed it up in a way I could understand: "Jesus steps in and absorbs all the wrath of God and restores favor to us."[38] I know what it felt like to be out of favor with God because of my sins, and there wasn't a thing I could do to justify myself. But when I gave my heart to the Lord before that summer in Texas I felt the weight of my sin wash away, even though it took me a while to comprehend it intellectually. One of the greatest joys in life is to suddenly feel clean before the Lord, justified by Him alone, so that Satan has lost all ground to accuse us. But I'll warn you, the evil one doesn't give up accusing easily, and sometimes we cooperate by reminding ourselves of past sins or despairing when we fail again in some new way. (Even Peter denied Jesus three times!) So I'll let you in on a secret. There's a reason why I have a colorful picture of a bunch of hyssop hanging in my prayer room, and it's not for aesthetics. Under that photo I have the words, "Psalm 51." It's there because I need to remind myself:

"Purify me with hyssop, and I shall be clean; wash me and I shall be whiter than snow.... Create in me a clean heart, O God, and renew a steadfast spirit within me. Do not cast me away from Your presence and do not take Your Holy Spirit from me. Restore to me the joy of Your salvation and sustain me with a willing spirit.... Deliver me from bloodguiltiness, O God, the God of my salvation; then my tongue will joyfully sing of Your righteousness.... For You do not delight in sacrifice, otherwise I would give it; You are not pleased with burnt offering. The sacrifices of God are a broken spirit; a broken and contrite heart, O God, You will not despise." (Psalm 51:7, 10-12, 14(a), 16-17)

---

[38] Pastor Patrick Bowler, Valley Life Church, Lebanon, Oregon, live-streaming sermon entitled, *In A Single Day,* 3/29/20, valleylifechurch.net

But if you really want to disarm the accuser, put on truth (Ephesians 6:10-20). How can an accusation stick when we say, "Yep, it's true; but I'm a sinner saved by grace."

Grace is unmerited favor, extended because Jesus took the punishment we were due. A just God cannot just look the other way at sin. Someone had to pay for our sin. So Jesus did it for us, on the cross. Why would He do that? His great, unfathomable love for His kids, His lost sheep! And all we have to do is "repent" [change our minds] and believe in the gospel."[39] Those are Jesus' own words! Pretty simple?

Earlier on I thought I was a basically good person, or a "B.G.P.," as my late husband later described this mindset. He once gave a talk with that title at a seminar, and I sure wish I'd kept his notes. The gist of it was, we're not basically good. In the garden, everything God created *was* good, including the first man and woman. "Very good,"[40] in fact! But after the fall, we were not good. We were in rebellion against God. Mankind became so wicked that God wiped out all creation except one man, Noah, who "found favor in the eyes of the Lord,"[41] and his family. Out of compassion, God gave mankind a new start through that family. But if you read the entire Old Testament you'll see God's patience and great mercy put to the test again and again. You'll see the great lengths He went to for His rebellious people, and their constant cycle of judgment, repentance, and falling right back down. The Law, and the judges, and the kings, and the prophets were sent, but mankind could not fix our own sin problem.

Back before I understood all this I thought I could earn my way into heaven by good works; but no human being can. So God our Father sent His only Son to take our sins upon Himself,

---

[39] Mark 1:15

[40] Genesis 1:31

[41] Genesis 6:8

make Himself, the sinless "Lamb of God,"[42] an offering for our sin. As a result, we can take on His righteousness, and shed our sins and our attempts at self-righteousness like filthy rags,[43] becoming new, redeemed sons and daughters of God. He restores our souls! Look what God said through the prophet Isaiah:

" 'Come now, and let us reason together,' says the Lord, 'Though your sins are as scarlet, they will be white as snow; though they are red like crimson, they will be like wool.' " (Isaiah 1:18) (Like a lamb's wool!)

---

[42] John 1:29

[43] Isaiah 64:6

B. "He guides me in paths of righteousness for His name's sake."[44]

(Photo by Emily Ruckert)

After He restores our souls, the Lord doesn't waste any time putting us on track, guiding us away from the things that will pull us right back, and nearer to the places where we can grow. Some call it formation. That summer in Dallas I started telling you about earlier was my formation. Formation, or a period of early growth, isn't always fun, and mine wasn't at times. I had for most of my life been practically paralyzed with shyness. Being thrust in a miniature, dorm-style apartment with three other girls from all different walks of life was an eye-opener. One of my roommates was straight off the hippy commune, another was the daughter of a Baptist preacher, and the third

---

[44] Psalm 23:3

was a Catholic girl who'd been baptized in the Spirit all by herself when she was in middle school. This occurred before anyone, herself included, even knew what it meant, and she was also miraculously healed. (She was genuine!)

I'm debating whether to tell you the story of how I landed at the Bible college in the first place. What I mean is, what drew me there. I guess I will, but it involves backtracking.

That close call with the bikers wasn't the last of my bad experiences. You know how they say, "If you play with fire long enough you're going to get burned." Well, I did. But that's not what drew me to the Lord. His love that I saw in others and read about in His Word is what coaxed me out of darkness into His dazzling light until I simply said yes to Jesus. When I did, He filled me with His Spirit and I experienced the Lord's love in a way that I have never to this day been able to find words to describe. There aren't any. Human words, human experience, aren't even in the same universe with His kind of love. I fell so deeply in love with Jesus, the Shepherd of my soul, that I practically inhaled the Bible and any other spiritual literature I could get my hands on. I was, as the Scripture indicates, a new creation in Christ, which meant old things had to fall away.[45]

At first I tried to include my friends, even some of the guys I dated, in my new life, practically dragging them to prayer meetings. But most of them just didn't want to leave behind the temporary pleasures of sin. And as I read Scriptures I realized there is no fellowship between light and darkness.[46] The first and only time after I became a Christian that I went back to that club where I'd hung out, it literally looked so dark, so empty, so dirty, as if my eyes had been blinded and suddenly I could see. I couldn't wait to get out. So part of what the Lord led me to do was get out of the environment and the relationships that had led me to sin and would tempt me all over again. That is just

---

[45] 2nd Corinthians 5:17

[46] 1st Letter of John 1:3-7 and 2nd Corinthians 6:14-18

part of the story of how I ended up in Dallas that summer at a Bible college.

He just kept leading me in His paths, His righteousness, *not mine*.

And you know what? When we stay on the path a while, it gets easier and easier to walk in God's ways, to follow His lead. Look what David's son Solomon wrote:

"But the path of the righteous is like the light of dawn, that shines brighter and brighter until the full day." (Prov. 4:18)

That doesn't mean we can't trip up. But...

"Therefore let him who thinks he stands take heed that he does not fall. No temptation has overtaken you but such as is common to man; and God is faithful, who will not allow you to be tempted beyond what you are able, but with the temptation will provide the way of escape also, so that you will be able to endure it." (1st Corinthians 10:12-13)

Can you bear with one more of my stories? As a brand-new Christian I was walking strong, but suddenly my old boyfriend came back from Wyoming, hoping to take up where we'd left off when I was a heathen. He took me to a place where I wouldn't normally have gone, where temptation was lurking. In the parking lot, late at night when no one should have been out there, a guy in a wheelchair called over to my ex asking him about his motorcycle. This young man (about our age) told us before he was paralyzed he used to have a Harley, and they engaged in friendly motorcycle banter. As it turned out, *miraculously,* he was from a Bible college in Texas, and he'd come to Maryland on tour with the group I then noticed was hanging around a bus with the name Christ for the Nations Institute on it. I was stunned. When my sister had recently given me their magazine, I'd noticed on the back that they were starting sign-ups for their six-week, summer Bible school program. I'd been, in the back of my mind, contemplating signing up, but I was scared. Seeing that singing group there late at night, stopped to rest from their journey, I knew without even a smidgen of doubt that God was calling me. It was way too bizarre, running into someone from Dallas in a remote area of Maryland, from the exact school I was thinking about going to. That realization gave me the courage to say no to temptation. I made it clear to my ex-boyfriend I wanted to go home and got back on the bike.

Obviously, from all the stories I've dumped on you, you can probably figure out I also filled out the form for the Bible college and got on the plane not much later. If we're truly His, and not faking it, our Shepherd will go to whatever lengths He has to in order to keep us.

This section of a favorite psalm describes the process God works in us to lead us and keep us on the right path:

"Delight yourself in the Lord; and He will give you the desires of your heart. Commit your way to the Lord, trust also in Him, and He will do it. He will bring forth your righteousness as the light, and your judgment as the noonday. Rest in the Lord and wait patiently for Him." (Psalm 37:4-7(a))

This process is known as sanctification, and it lasts a lifetime. It means that as we spend time with the Lord, praying and in His Word, we gradually take on more of the Lord's attributes, His character, His ways. It's kind of like the way a pearl is formed by rubbing against the inside of an oyster, eventually turning into something quite beautiful to behold. But note in Psalm 37 (above) the last line quoted reads, "Rest in the Lord and wait patiently." When I was first learning sign language, I walked out after class talking with my instructor and he pointed out to me a bumper sticker on his car. It read, "Be patient. God isn't finished with me yet.'' That's a reminder to us to be patient with ourselves, as well as with others who may not know church lingo or how to follow along in their Bibles, and who might say and do things that are a little shocking. Be patient; God's on the case, and He's very patient.

So if He's leading us on His paths, how hard is it to follow? That depends on what we're used to.

Long after my first husband died, when my kids were raised, God blessed me to no end with my wonderful husband Dave. He captured my heart with his patience and selflessness and the audacious guts it took to take me on! The whole online romance, Dave wooing me from 3,000 miles away, was quite the act of God. After we'd been married about five years, both Dave's parents had major heart surgeries in close succession, so we decided to move to Oregon to help take care of them. After Dave's tender-hearted yet strong mom passed, we were the primary caregivers for Dad.

When it was getting closer to the end for Dad, yet he refused hospice, I was deeply troubled as our trip to Maryland to see my kids approached. Dad wasn't doing well. He was in an assisted living place by then, and Dave's siblings were going to be around part of the time. But as much as I wanted desperately to see my family back east, I was deeply distressed at leaving Dad. He'd had a spill on his bright red electric scooter just shortly before, landing him in the hospital. But he was back at the care facility the day before we were to take off, and we visited him. I had a real heart-to-heart with him when Dave was out of the room, but still the next morning after church when we were preparing to hit the road for a 3,000-mile road trip to Maryland my heart was breaking. So I'd written Dad a letter (during church, which is unusual for me, but some of the sermon figured into what I wrote). I had a feeling we'd never see Dad again. But my Dave knew how much I needed to see my kids, and how worn out I was from caring for Dad, so he refused to cancel the trip. We swung by Brookdale where Dad lived and I ran up to the reception desk and gave the attendant my note for Dad. I didn't have the courage to take it up to his room, because I knew I wouldn't have the heart to leave. I found out later Dad had snuck off again on his scooter to go to church (at 95 and very sick!) when I'd come by, so I wouldn't have found him in his room even if I'd gone up. But here's some of what I told my father-in-law in my note, that pertains to one of the primary attributes of sheep: they're good followers. This is from my scribbled notes that I hung onto after I composed Dad's note, and it's probably not exactly how it ultimately ended up because I'm a compulsive editor. After expressing how much we loved him and how hard it was to leave, I told him I'd recently been thinking of what it meant for Jesus' apostles who were fishermen to leave everything behind including their nets when He made the call to them, "Follow Me." I knew Dad was facing death, and I knew he had to leave behind the safety net of this world and everything and everyone he loved and venture out into "deep waters." So I told Dad about how Jesus just simply calls us to follow Him (not clean ourselves up, or get everything in order on our own). I reminded him of how he and Mom were such good dancers. He'd given us a picture recently of the two of them dancing together at a dance hall when they were young, and we had it prominently displayed. But I tried to explain that for a couple to flow together well, one had to be the leader and one had to be the follower. All his life Dad had been the leader, and Mom the follower. And he was good at it. They were both good at their roles. (Mom was such a good wife!) But Mom had gone home to be with the Lord, and I told Dad it was his turn to be the follower. Time to let Jesus be in charge, let Jesus call the shots, and lead him all the way home. I don't know what Dad's reaction was, because he passed away shortly after we arrived in Maryland. But I hope he had a good dance home.

Irises Dad dug up from his yard for me to plant in ours.

But here's the primary way I believe the Great Shepherd keeps us "sheepy" followers on His path: His Word. It's His roadmap and guidebook, His personal love letter to us. If you're not that familiar yet with the Bible, I'd recommend you find a good study Bible. I wish I'd had one in the beginning, because there's a lot of basic stuff they didn't teach me in Catholic school growing up about God's Word.

4. "Even though I walk through the valley of the shadow of death, I fear no evil, for You are with me; Your rod and Your staff, they comfort me." (Ps. 23:4)

This is a tough one to walk through, even to imagine walking through, if you haven't yet. I don't want to minimize or sugarcoat it.

Whether it's you yourself or a loved one facing death, when it first hits it can be like a dark, foreboding cloud hovering over you that you want to run from. I can still remember getting the news that my first husband had cancer, and just lying beside him sobbing, weeping until I could weep no more.

This is way too deep to lay out here, but the Lord prepared me internally far in advance for my late husband's death. Some people have no warning, no time to say goodbye. Others who watch their loved ones suffer for a very long time still grieve. Maybe it's slightly easier to say goodbye when we believe they're shedding their wasted bodies and going where there's no more suffering, no more tears;[47] but still it's hard. I felt a lot like that with my father-in-law who died at 95. But I can't fathom what it's like facing death for yourself or another who doesn't know Jesus. The truth is, only God can read hearts; so we mostly just don't know what goes on inside a person in those last seconds before they step out of this life and into one or the other, eternal life, or the stark opposite. That sounds way too blunt, doesn't it? But those are the options, heaven or hell. Still there's mercy, if we don't wait until our hearts get too hard to swallow our pride:

"There were those who dwelt in darkness and in the shadow of death, prisoners in misery and chains, because they had rebelled against the words of God and spurned the counsel of the Most High. Therefore He humbled their heart with labor; they stumbled and there was none to help. Then they cried out to the Lord in their trouble; He saved them out of their distresses. He brought them out of darkness and the shadow of death and broke their bands apart. Let them give thanks to the Lord for His lovingkindness, and for His wonders to the sons of men!"[48]

That, my loved ones, is good news for the humble.

If you're right now facing this valley, or watching someone you care deeply for face it, my heart goes out to you! I've been there, losing my husband when I was 38, then not long afterward being the one to find my father dead.

Yet there is a light in this tunnel, and it's contained right in the second part of the verse: "Even though I walk through the valley of the shadow of death, *I fear no evil, for You are with me; Your rod and Your staff they comfort me.*" (Verse 4 of 23rd Psalm, emphasis mine)

---

[47] Revelation 21:3-4

[48] Psalm 107:10-15

(Photo courtesy of Emily Ruckert.)

He is with you! Remember at Christmas we sing, "O Come, O Come, Emmanuel"? What does Emmanuel mean, but "God with us"! He does not require us to walk this path alone. You don't need to fear evil or darkness or the deepest chasm. The Shepherd of our souls walks with us! And He walks us home, if we're His.

After rising from the dead Jesus said, "...lo, I am with you always, even to the end of the age."[49] Today in some circles that outdated word, "lo," (above) would probably be translated, "Yo, dude!" You have to have a little urban background like I do to appreciate that though.

There is one place where only Christ can accompany us, and it's that final journey home. You've surely read the obituaries about the person who passed away "surrounded by friends and family." I spent the last five days of my husband Danny's life with him in the hospital, night and day, barely taking time to eat. His father and sister and brother were there as often as they could possibly be. But I was determined not to leave his side, because I knew he was scared to die alone. Even for a mighty man of God like my husband Danny, there was still some fear

[49] Matthew 28:20

of the unknown at first. I only remember twice in that five-day period drifting off for, oh, fifteen minutes or so, and then abruptly startling myself awake when I realized I'd fallen asleep. Honestly, I thought I was going to die right there beside my husband, I was so far beyond exhausted! But he'd never asked for much of anything from me, and he'd been so strong, injecting himself in the abdomen with the heparin (blood thinner) he needed because he knew it was too hard for me. Never complaining.

Yet after all that, I couldn't cross over the threshold to death with him. That part of the journey Jesus alone walked him through, even though I was there in the hospital room. The last words I remember Danny saying were, "I love Jesus," and he spoke them with a combination of sincerity and tenderness I have never witnessed in anyone, ever. He had stopped breathing once before that and I went into a panic screaming, "Danny, breathe!" And he did. But not too much later he asked for a pencil and pen, by gestures, because he was too weak to speak very loudly. He was so close to the finish line his writing was almost illegible, but his family and I deciphered it. He'd written, "If Jesus calls me home, I need your permission to say yes." Danny had made it clear in writing, before his last hospital stay, he didn't want heavy meds, only Tylenol with codeine if things got bad. But mostly he wasn't in pain except for the catheter, which the nurse had a solution to (though it took away a little more of his dignity). But that was okay with him. Danny was one of the most humble men I've ever known (it was one of the things I admired most about him). So he was in his right mind, able to think even if he couldn't speak. And the words Danny wrote cut us to the quick — utterly broke us. But yes, we agreed. (The kids weren't there, of course. Danny didn't want them to see him like that.) It wasn't very long at all after his request when Jesus did call Danny home. And this time I kept my mouth shut and called the nurse. But his spirit had already departed before she came; he was home. The Shepherd of our souls who walks with us all our days absolutely does not leave us orphaned when we cross over to death. So fear not, He's with us all the way!

And He's with the loved ones left behind. My kids are incredible, after all they've been through, by God's transforming grace. The depth of character forged in them through God working good out of adverse circumstances is unbelievable. I am so proud of them. Talk about fortitude! When you've been through losing your dad when you're young, God uses it to build strength and character in you. I think if anyone can make it through this current coronavirus nightmare, and still help others along the way, they can. When you've been down and out, you can let it turn you bitter, or you can have a heart for others in dire circumstances.

Here's an example. When my middle son Tommy was a young boy, a stranger came up and asked if he could borrow Tommy's bike to show him how to do wheelies. My trusting son didn't hesitate to hand over his shiny, fairly new bike. As Tommy stood by, the kid rode off, never to be seen again! Tom could have been permanently hardened by some things like that which happened to him growing up. But instead now that he's grown, I hear (second hand, not from him) of his selfless acts of kindness. I know that sort of a turnaround can only happen by God's grace working through us to forgive.

And here's an instance where God worked adversity for good, full cycle. My oldest son Dan had a car that was broken down and sat in our yard for years. One morning when we lived in Laurel, Maryland, I woke up and Dan greeted me with, "Now don't be alarmed that there's a guy in my car." He went on to tell me how he'd been at the gas station the night before and seen a homeless man and offered him his car (in our yard) to sleep in to come out of the cold. And, ironically, you won't believe what happened years later! When Dan was walking home late at night from his restaurant job in Baltimore, a group of hoodlums started to beat him up since they couldn't find any money on him, and who do you think came to Dan's rescue? A homeless guy who piped up to the muggers, “Hey, leave him alone! He just gave me his last dollar!” (The homeless man wasn’t making that up either.) And they did. God again and again works good out of all things, even catastrophes, for His children. Even what looked like the worst defeat of all time, God turned around for our greatest victory ever on the cross:

“Now I say this, brethren, that flesh and blood cannot inherit the kingdom of God; nor does the perishable inherit the imperishable.... But when this perishable will have put on the imperishable, and this mortal will have put on immortality, then will come about the saying that is written, ‘DEATH IS SWALLOWED UP in victory. O DEATH, WHERE IS YOUR VICTORY? O DEATH, WHERE IS YOUR STING?’ The sting of death is sin, and the power of sin is the law; but thanks be to God, who gives us the victory through our Lord Jesus Christ.”[50]

What about *the rod and the staff* in this verse, implements used by shepherds?

How does a rod function and how could it ever bring us comfort, especially when death is near?

I guess it makes a difference whose hands these implements are in. In this case, it’s the Good Shepherd, Jesus, wielding them. So we believe He only uses His rod for our good. Remember this Scripture from Chapter 2?

“And we know that God causes all things to work together for good to those who love God, to those who are called according to His purpose.” (Romans 8:28)

I know it because I’ve walked with Him 44 years and He’s never been anything but faithful and good, merciful and just. Not once.

---

[50] 1st Corinthians 15:50 & 54-57

What does a shepherd use his rod for? Correction, discipline, fighting off predators too perhaps?

Those are some of the functions a good shepherd takes seriously. A parent similarly has to discipline and correct his or her children to tame their obstinate self-will and defiance, protect them from harm, and most of all to teach them. Scripture states: “The rod and reproof give wisdom, but a child who gets his own way brings shame to his mother.” (Proverbs 29:15)

However, discipline has to be measured and administered in love, not in rage. I wasn't the perfect parent by far; I didn't always step back and wait until my anger had simmered down. And more than once harsh words slipped out of my mouth over the course of parenting my four children. Even when I immediately tried to take it back, the damage was done. I'm so, so sorry for that! Unfortunately, no parent is perfect, except our Heavenly Father. But children and parents have a lot of forgiving to do.

By the time my kids were all teens or approaching teen years (being so close together in age), I was really struggling to maintain order and discipline as a single parent. I did desperate things, like hoisting a heavy TV on my back and shoving it in the trunk of my car after the kids wouldn't turn it off when I told them to. I signed up for home security, but not to keep intruders out; rather, it was to keep my kids from sneaking out at night. And, of course, one of my more techie kids disabled it. (The downside of having four very bright kids.) He's probably the one who thwarted my parental controls program I put on our computer too, unless I never installed it right (which wouldn't surprise me).

I remember putting my teenagers on restriction for whatever infraction they'd committed so many times it was ridiculous, and I'd taken away so many privileges there was nothing left (nothing reasonable left anyway) to take away. Reasoning with them didn't work when the boys became taller than me and took on deep, booming voices. If I were a shepherd, I would not call myself a good one. I was overwhelmed as a single parent of four and fell short in many ways.

Does God correct you? He sure corrects me; and I'm mighty glad for it! Sometimes it's a gentle, or not so gentle, nudge through His Word; other times He uses another person (like my sister). Do we like it at the time? No way! But it pays off for us in the long run: "All discipline for the moment seems not to be joyful, but sorrowful; yet to those who have been trained by it, afterwards it yields the peaceful fruit of righteousness." (Hebrews 12:11) My sister Jeanie tried to get that into my thick skull when my very precocious firstborn was fairly young, and I thought it was too soon to apply. Next thing I knew I had four kids that weren't properly trained in discipline.

My son Stephen asked me recently if I had a problem with money management when I told him we'd only had $7 in savings when his father died. I tried to defend myself. But after he hung up I thought, *yeah, I did have a problem; but it wasn't with money management per se*. I didn't spend hardly anything on myself, didn't gamble, and was pretty frugal in most things. A lot of our funding went toward Christian education; and I don't regret that. But the real problem with my overspending came when my kids were teenagers, and I didn't know how to say no to fast food. Part of parenting and of good shepherding is setting boundaries and saying, "No, you can't go over this line," and enforcing it.

And our shepherd is always good, always fair, always loving. He never fails. If you've ever read the love chapter, 1st Corinthians 13, the Shepherd of our souls epitomizes that kind of love. [51] He's patient and kind, not self-centered. He doesn't rejoice in unrighteousness or want to see others fall. He not only

---

[51] 1st Corinthians 13:4-8

doesn't "take into account a wrong suffered,"[52] He did the suffering *for* our wrongs.

David the shepherd-psalmist knew something about the rod. It was a tool of his trade, but it was also symbolic of the discipline he himself received when he went astray. Many of us have heard the story of David's great sin with Bathsheba, another man's wife whom he lusted after when he spied her bathing below his rooftop perch. He was king by then, and he could get most anything he wanted. So he sent for this beautiful woman he'd not turned his eyes away from, and he slept with her. Things went from bad to worse when she told him she was pregnant, while her husband was out fighting battles for David. David tried all kinds of conniving to bring her husband back from battle so he'd think it was his child. But her husband Uriah was a loyal soldier and refused to enjoy intimacy with his wife while the rest of his men were risking their lives in the battlefield. So David sunk even deeper into depravity and had his right-hand man send Uriah directly out on the front lines. When the battle heated up to its fiercest, he had his men withdraw, deliberately leaving Uriah to die. About the equivalent of hiring a hitman to do your dirty work. Our sweet psalmist who wrote the 23rd Psalm! Yeah, if you've never read the story[53] it's worth reading.

But God sent a prophet named Nathan to confront David, to correct the shepherd God had appointed king over Israel. Even though David then admitted his sin and God forgave Him, there were serious consequences for David. Nathan told David, "The Lord also has taken away your sin; you shall not die. However, because by this deed you have given occasion to the enemies of the Lord to blaspheme, the child also that is born to you shall surely die." (2nd Samuel 12:13-14).

God didn't just leave David in his sin, He shepherded him with the rod of correction. He disciplined him severely. A just

---

[52] 1st Corinthians 13:5

[53] 2nd Samuel 11:1-27

God can't look the other way at our sins, or we'll die in them and never repent. Sin separates us from God until we repent, and it's not a fun state of affairs trying to cover up our sins. If you really want to see David's torment of soul while he was carrying around his secret sins and the subsequent forgiveness, read all of Psalm 38, but here's a sampling from it:

"O Lord, rebuke me not in your wrath, and chasten me not in your burning anger.... For my iniquities are gone over my head; as a heavy burden they weigh too much for me. My wounds grow foul and fester because of my folly. I am bent over and greatly bowed down; I go mourning all day long.... My heart throbs, my strength fails me; and the light of my eyes, even that has gone from me.... For I am ready to fall, and my sorrow is continually before me. For I confess my iniquity; I am full of anxiety because of my sin."[54]

Does he sound like a happy sinner? The rod of correction brings comfort, reconciliation. If we've lived in right relationship with the Lord, we shouldn't be tormented when we near the home stretch. If He could forgive David, He can forgive us when we come to Him and ask.

God is God. He knew in advance what David was going to do with Bathsheba before he did it, yet God called David, "a man after My heart."[55] And He had forgiven David so completely that He allowed our Messiah's lineage to come straight through the line of David. That's how great God's forgiveness is. This is from one of David's many psalms:

"As far as the east is from the west, so far has He removed our transgressions from us. Just as a father has compassion on his children, so the Lord has compassion on those who fear Him."[56]

---

[54] Psalm 38:1, 4-6, 10, 17-18

[55] 1st Samuel 13:14 and Acts 13:22

[56] Psalm 103:12-13

That part of above Scripture about God the Father's compassion through His loving discipline is echoed in Paul's letter to the Hebrews:

"...God deals with you as with sons; for what son is there whom his father does not discipline? But if you are without discipline, of which all have become partakers, then you are illegitimate children and not sons."[57]

Sometimes we need a graphic illustration to bring home the reality that He disciplines us because we *are* precious sons and daughters of our Father, even if the rest of the world views us differently.

---

[57] Hebrews 12:7-8

Jesus said, “All that the Father gives Me will come to Me, and the one who comes to Me I will certainly not cast out.” (John 6:37) You can count on that.

And what about the staff David refers to in this part of the 23rd Psalm? How could it bring comfort?

Have you ever hiked mountains high enough to require a walking stick? My husband Dave and his father and brothers were mountain climbers. His brother Scott even wrote a book about his mountain climbing exploits.[58] Scott was a serious

---

[58] Scott Schmidt, Friends of the Abyss, with excerpts from the climbing log of Bob Richards (Deer Harbor, WA: SCHMIDDLEARTH PRESS, 2011). Used with permission.

climber until he lost his hiking partner to a fall on one of their climbs. But my husband's dad was still hiking into his early 90's. By this time, though, he required a walking stick to maneuver the ascent and descent, and he wasn't attempting the higher elevations.

I liken the shepherd's staff to that walking stick used for support, even though it had many more purposes. When a shepherd wasn't strong enough, was pressing on through pain as he labored, or was just plain weary, it helped hold him up. Our Shepherd, our God, does that. He steadies us, and He rights us when we're close to falling, like the shepherd's staff does: "The Lord supports the afflicted…." (Psalm 147:6)

In David's day the shepherd's staff or crook had a little curled end, so it could be used to pull back the straying sheep, or get them out of the tangled spot they were stuck in. Our God does that too. Life is a little like a precipice, and He keeps us "on the path," as the saying goes. I like this spiritual image:

"The steps of a man are established by the Lord, and He delights in his way. When he falls, he will not be hurled headlong, because the Lord is the One who holds his hand." (Psalm 37:23-24)

Did you notice it didn't say, "if he falls"? We all fall; but I can picture Him gently extending His shepherd's staff to help us get back up. And that comforts me. Do you see the tenderness of the Lord our Shepherd in the end of that verse above? He holds our hand! Our God is a gentle shepherd. Speaking of gentleness, have you ever read the parable Jesus told of the lost sheep, where the shepherd leaves the 99 and goes out after one stray? When he finds it, what do you think the shepherd does? He "lays it on his shoulders, rejoicing." (Luke 15:5)

Emily Ruckert is pictured below, in an unrehearsed demonstration of a good shepherd's love.

(Photo courtesy of Emily Ruckert)

Do you enjoy music? There's a beautiful, ancient hymn entitled, "The King of Love My Shepherd Is." A variety of modern renditions exist. If you're a music lover, I think you'll find it an inspiring, artistic representation of the shepherd motif in the 23rd Psalm.

5. "You prepare a table before me in the presence of my enemies; You have anointed my head with oil; My cup overflows." (Ps. 23:5)

Well, we talked a bit about this in the beginning, so let's look at this table. It can have a lot of symbolic meaning, but let's start with the literal meaning: a table is the place where we receive sustenance, provisions for our bodies. Our God provides for our bodily needs. When Jesus' disciples asked Him to teach them how to pray, part of what has become known as the Lord's Prayer was included in this, "... Our Father who is in heaven, hallowed be Your name. Your kingdom come. Your will be done, on earth as it is in heaven. Give us this day our daily bread."[59]

Jesus also offered spiritual food at a table. He called together His closest followers, His apostles, and they gathered together around the table He'd had them prepare for Him. "And He said to them, 'I have earnestly desired to eat this Passover with you before I suffer; for I say to you, I shall never again eat it until it is fulfilled in the kingdom of God.' "[60]

---

[59] Matthew 6:9-11

[60] Luke 22:15-16

Wow, do we really get that? This final meal before His crucifixion was the fulfillment of the first Passover, when the Israelites offered an "unblemished"[61] lamb as a sacrifice, so that the angel of death would pass over them. The Egyptians' firstborn sons were all wiped out as judgment for their refusal to obey God and let His people go free from enslavement.[62] But the Israelites were spared. This unblemished lamb foreshadowed Jesus, the sinless Lamb of God[63] who was slain for our sins, so we'd be passed over for the judgment we were due for our sins. He became the sacrifice that freed us from the slavery of sin and death!

Getting back to the last supper:

"And when He had taken some bread and given thanks, He broke it and gave it to them, saying, 'This is My body which is given for you; do this in remembrance of Me.' And in the same way He took the cup after they had eaten, saying, 'This cup which is poured out for you is the new covenant in My blood.' "[64]

Anyone who's partaken of communion in a traditional church has heard these words. But have we listened to their meaning? I think growing up I heard those words so often I took them for granted. But while at Bible college in Dallas, they especially came alive when I had no car on campus. I was afraid to join my roommates at a church denomination I didn't feel comfortable with, and the church I wanted to attend was too far to walk to. So I lay on my bunk bed in our empty apartment and cried. I felt so broken being unable to worship my Lord and take communion with other believers. The next week a roommate felt sorry for me and lent me her car, so I drove alone into the

---

[61] Exodus 12:5

[62] Exodus 12:1-30

[63] John 1:29

[64] Luke 22:19-20

city to church from then on. And my heart leapt for joy! Oh, to be among God's children again, receiving communion together! Maybe you have to first feel the absence to fully feel the joy. But that deep, communal fellowship at the table of the Lord with other people who believe is like no other friendship. It's described in the First Letter of John:

"If we say that we have fellowship with Him [God] and yet walk in the darkness, we lie and do not practice the truth; but if we walk in the Light[65] as He Himself is in the Light, we have fellowship with one another, and the blood of Jesus His Son cleanses us from all sin."[66]

(If this part about light isn't making sense to you, follow the footnote embedded in the middle of above quote to get a clearer view.)

And just as in this 5th verse of the 23rd Psalm the table was prepared "in the presence of my enemies," so too was Jesus' last supper: "But behold," Jesus said, "the hand of the one betraying Me is with Mine on the table."[67] How could anyone deny the 23rd Psalm (like a multitude of prophecies in the Old Testament, especially the Book of Isaiah) was fulfilled in Jesus?

(And there's another table coming at the end of time which we'll talk about with the last verse of Psalm 23.)

In that passage discussed earlier when Jesus directs our attention to persistent prayer for our physical needs, He also addresses our spiritual needs:

"So I say to you, ask, and it will be given to you; seek, and you will find; knock, and it will be opened to you. For everyone who asks, receives; and he who seeks, finds; and to him who

---

[65] John 1:4-9; John 8:12; Ephesians 5:7-13

[66] 1st Letter of John 1:6-7

[67] Luke 22:21

knocks, it will be opened. Now suppose one of you fathers is asked by his son for a fish; he will not give him a snake instead of a fish, will he? Or if he is asked for an egg, he will not give him a scorpion, will he? If you then, being evil, know how to give good gifts to your children, how much more will your heavenly Father give the Holy Spirit to those who ask Him?" (Luke 11:9-13)

See the part at the end about the Holy Spirit? Well, that ties right in with the last part of verse 5 of Psalm 23:

"You have anointed my head with oil; my cup overflows."[68]

Oil is one of the emblems or symbols which represent the Holy Spirit. It is the Holy Spirit, the third person of the Trinity, who seals us for His kingdom and anoints us:

"In Him, you also, after listening to the message of truth, the gospel of your salvation — having also believed, you were sealed in Him with the Holy Spirit of promise, who is given as a pledge of our inheritance, with a view to the redemption of God's own possession, to the praise of His glory." (Ephesians 1:13-14)

That seal the Holy Spirit places on us is remotely like an engagement ring a man puts on his bride-to-be. That ring is supposed to be the groom's guarantee that in the future they will come together as man and wife. The Holy Spirit places His seal, His pledge, on believers guaranteeing that those who have responded to Jesus' offer will indeed come to spend eternal life with Him when this life ends.

Oil is also a symbol of God's anointing. In the Old Testament, specific instructions were given on "making a holy anointing oil,"[69] and it was used to anoint and consecrate the tent of

---

[68] Psalm 23:5

[69] Exodus 30:31

meeting and the ark of the testimony and everything inside, as well as the priests, signifying holiness.[70] When Saul was anointed as the first king of Israel, "Samuel took the flask of oil, poured it on his head, kissed him and said, 'Has not the Lord anointed you a ruler over His inheritance?' "[71] After anointing Saul, Samuel said, "Then the Spirit of the Lord will come upon you mightily, and you shall prophesy with them [a group of prophets] and be changed into another man."[72]

And that's exactly what happened. The oil was like an outward sign of the Holy Spirit being poured out on him. In the New Testament people were anointed ceremonially with oil too. The apostles whom Jesus sent out to minister were, "casting out many demons and were anointing with oil many sick people and were healing them."[73] Those things that they did (i.e., prophesying in Old Testament reference; and in the New Testament, healing and the distinguishing of spirits, which was a prerequisite to casting out demons) are listed among the gifts of the Spirit in 1st Corinthians 12:1-12. And "there are varieties of gifts, but the same Spirit,"[74] and "each one is given the manifestation of the Spirit for the common good."[75]

Jesus' disciples were like sheep without a shepherd, running scared, at the time of His death. But after Jesus rose from the dead He instructed His apostles to stay in Jerusalem, waiting until the Father's promise He'd told them about was fulfilled.[76] Jesus said, "John baptized with water, but you will be baptized with the Holy Spirit not many days from now."[77]

---

[70] Exodus 30:25-31

[71] 1st Samuel 10:1

[72] 1st Samuel 10:6

[73] Mark 6:13

[74] 1st Corinthians 12:4

[75] 1st Corinthians 12:7

[76] Acts 1:4, Luke 24:49

[77] Acts 1:5

And it happened just as Jesus said it would. It was phenomenal! A sound "like a violent, rushing wind"[78] filled the house, and "tongues as of fire... rested on each of them."[79] Then they were filled with the Holy Spirit, and unlearned men suddenly began speaking in unknown tongues, and, remarkably, the crowd outside from all different nations each heard them speaking in their own native language.[80] It was like the reverse of the tower of Babel incident in the Old Testament. In Babel (later called Babylon) God confused the people's universal language when they arrogantly tried to build a tower to heaven, causing them to no longer understand one another.[81] Only at Pentecost, instead of people being divided by a language barrier, they were brought together by language. A miraculous act of God caused people of every nation gathered for the feast to simultaneously understand a foreign tongue in their own language. The people were "astonished."[82]

Afterward Peter, freshly baptized with the Holy Spirit,[83] boldly spoke out to the crowd gathered outside, explaining that what they'd just witnessed was the fulfillment of the prophecy given by Joel. The book of Joel found in the Bible is estimated to have been written anywhere from 400-900 years before Christ.[84] Peter said, "For these men are not drunk, as you suppose, for it is *only* the third hour of the day; but this is what was spoken of through the prophet Joel:

---

[78] Acts 2:2

[79] Acts 2:3

[80] Acts 2:4-6

[81] Genesis 11:1-9

[82] Acts 2:7

[83] Acts 1:5 and 2:4

[84] *The ESV Study Bible, English Standard Version* (ESV) (Wheaton, Illinois: Crossway, a publishing ministry of Good News Publishers, 2007) Pg. 1643

'AND IT SHALL BE IN THE LAST DAYS,' God says, 'THAT I WILL POUR FORTH OF MY SPIRIT ON ALL MANKIND; AND YOUR SONS AND YOUR DAUGHTERS SHALL PROPHESY, AND YOUR YOUNG MEN SHALL SEE VISIONS, AND YOUR OLD MEN SHALL DREAM DREAMS; EVEN ON MY BONDSLAVES, BOTH MEN AND WOMEN, I WILL IN THOSE DAYS POUR FORTH OF MY SPIRIT and they shall prophesy. AND I WILL GRANT WONDERS IN THE SKY ABOVE AND SIGNS ON THE EARTH BELOW, BLOOD, AND FIRE, AND VAPOR OF SMOKE. THE SUN WILL BE TURNED INTO DARKNESS AND THE MOON INTO BLOOD, BEFORE THE GREAT AND GLORIOUS DAY OF THE LORD SHALL COME. AND IT SHALL BE THAT EVERYONE WHO CALLS ON THE NAME OF THE LORD WILL BE SAVED.' " [85]

When I was saved I was also baptized in the Holy Spirit. I think one of the more dramatic evidences of the Holy Spirit in my life was how the Lord took a shy girl and suddenly gave me this burning desire to boldly proclaim the gospel. I still fight shyness and I still fail, but I care more about God's children than I do about what they think of me. My heart was so hardened before I became a Christian I'd literally forgotten how to cry. Even at funerals. But what the Holy Spirit does on the inside of believers is to soften and transform our hearts.

Just like in the end of this verse ("You have anointed my head with oil; my cup overflows"),[86] The Holy Spirit is poured out liberally on us. Our cup overflows. Remember in the verse cited earlier that talks about asking God for gifts, and trusting He'll only give what's good for us, it concluded, "If you then, being evil, know how to give good gifts to your children, how much more will *your* heavenly Father give the Holy Spirit to those who ask Him?"[87] So trust Him, and don't be afraid to ask for His Holy Spirit. We are useless without His Spirit.

---

[85] Acts 2:15-21; and Joel 2:28-32

[86] Psalm 23:5

[87] Luke 11:13

But be wary of false prophets and false shepherds, such as those who falsify the gifts of the Spirit or try to feed you a watered-down version of God's Word. Your standard is the Word of God. If you know it, you can spot a counterfeit. Even we, God's little sheep, could be led astray. But don't get so paranoid that you're holed up in your room, afraid to try going to a church (like I did in Dallas). Just ask God to lead you.

Jesus told a parable about a Samaritan who found a "half-dead" and naked mugging victim and compassionately "bandaged up his wounds, pouring oil and wine on them." [88] A commentary I read[89] explained that the oil was used to mollify the wound (meaning to soothe, soften, make less intense) and to close it up and protect it from dirt and germs. Do you see why oil, with its soothing, comforting, and protecting properties, is seen as a symbol of the Holy Spirit? He does all those things for us. He softens our hearts (I feel that tenderizing of my heart so often!); and He will always be to me, my Comforter![90]

If you've got a good study Bible you can find many references in the concordance to various forms of the word, "comfort," showing how God comforts us in Scripture. But here's an example:

"So the church… enjoyed peace, being built up; and going on in the fear of the Lord and in the comfort of the Holy Spirit, it continued to increase." (Acts 9:31)

---

[88] Luke 10:30-34

[89] *New One Volume Edition, Commentary on the Whole Bible, by Matthew Henry*, Edited by Rev. Leslie Church, Ph.D., F.R. Hist S., (Grand Rapids, MI: Zondervan Publishing House, 1961), Pg. 1448

[90] John 14:26, taken from *The New Testament of Our Lord and Saviour Jesus Christ with Psalms and Proverbs,* commonly known as the Authorized (King James) Version, The Gideons International 1976 Edition (Philadelphia, PA: National Publishing Company, 1968), Pg. 215

And through His ever-present Spirit He protects us the way oil seals out dirt and germs. He really does, especially when we're still like baby sheep. As a new believer, I didn't have very good sense. I remember being so on fire for the Lord early on as a Christian that I picked up a great big hitchhiker right outside the University of Maryland where I was a student. I was hoping for an opportunity to share the gospel with him; and God kept me safe.

I certainly wouldn't be inclined to do that now, but it was almost like a honeymoon period where I was walking in a little cloud of protection from God as I grew wiser. So don't worry, God's got you! But…, Jesus did tell His disciples:

"Behold, I send you out as sheep in the midst of wolves; so be shrewd as serpents and innocent as doves." (Matthew 10:16)

6. "Surely goodness and lovingkindness will follow me all the days of my life, and I will dwell in the house of the Lord forever." (Ps. 23:6)

I love the word lovingkindness, because it's such a beautiful description of the way God melds love and kindness together in a way only He can. But since the word lovingkindness is more often interpreted as mercy in other translations I'm familiar with, let's primarily use the ESV translation for this first part of the verse: "Surely goodness and mercy shall follow me all the days of my life…."[91]

How could goodness and mercy follow us? Well, God is good.[92] Goodness emanates from Him and to us, just from being in His presence. I'll bet if it were possible to trace the origin of the word "good" all the way to before there was any

---

[91] *The ESV Study Bible, English Standard Version* (ESV) (Wheaton, Illinois: Crossway, a publishing ministry of Good News Publishers, 2007) Pg. 966

[92] Psalm 34:8

written language, we'd find the origin to be rooted in the name of God (though that's just my wild guess, based only on the spelling of the two words, nothing else). God is altogether good, no sin, no evil. Even when He disciplines us it's for our good. And mercy, well, He is the epitome of mercy! Instead of giving us the eternal punishment we deserved, and eternal separation from our God, He took our punishment upon Himself and extended mercy to anyone who would accept His free gift. But how can this goodness and mercy *follow us*?

Well, I almost hate to use this example, because I absolutely do not recommend the very grim fairytales my mother read to me when I was a child. No wonder I had nightmares! But if your poor, young psyche was already damaged by the story of Hansel and Gretel,[93] remember what they left behind so they could find their way home from the spooky woods? Breadcrumbs. Maybe this is stretching it, but to me that goodness and mercy that follows us is like a trail of breadcrumbs, not to show us the way home (heaven). If you're already truly following Jesus, you're already on that road. But to me, the morsels of goodness and mercy are for those following us, observing our lives, and for the next generation. Skeptics are watching us, wondering if we're the real deal. Hoping we are, but afraid. The genuine Christians I encountered early on saturated me with crumbs of goodness and mercy, drawing me to yearn for that manna from heaven: God's goodness and mercy! His lovingkindness!

Which brings us to the second part of this 6th and final verse of the 23rd Psalm:

"...and I will dwell in the house of the Lord forever."[94]

---

[93] Grimm's Household Tales, Translated from the German and Edited by Margaret Hunt, with an Introduction by Andrew Lang, in two Volumes — Vol. I (London: George Bell and Sons, 1905), Pages 62-69

[94] Psalm 23:6

Are you feeling confident yet that that's your destination?

Remember when we were talking about the table Jesus prepares for us, in the 5th verse of Psalm 23? Well, here's a glimpse of the table yet to come:

" 'Let us rejoice and be glad and give the glory to Him, for the marriage of the Lamb has come and His bride has made herself ready.' It was given to her to clothe herself in fine linen, bright *and* clean; for the fine linen is the righteous acts of the saints. Then he said to me, 'Write, "Blessed are those who are invited to the marriage supper of the Lamb." ' And he said to me, 'These are true words of God.' "[95]

The bride this Scripture refers to is the church. I've often felt like the closest approximation to our love relationship with the Lord in this earthly realm is marriage, with its covenant commitment and intimate knowledge of one another. So to me it makes sense for the Lord to view it the way that it's described in this final book of the Bible. What a stark contrast between the wedding feast in heaven, and all the horrors going on in the earth that immediately precede it in that final book of the Bible.

Right now as I'm writing this book we're in the throes of the global COVID-19 (coronavirus) pandemic of 2020. The pandemonium has been startling, as the death toll rises and stocks plunge. Even Great Britain's Prime Minister has contracted the virus and was just released from the intensive care unit as I write. Fear, suspicion, and loneliness are mounting for those who are housebound, and I can't even imagine what it's like to be homeless in this crisis. (God be with them!) Hospitals and morgues are overrun, with not enough staff to take care of patients, along with an extreme shortage of medical equipment and hospital beds. Some people are hoarding surgical masks, and there are scarcities of essentials like soap and hand sanitizer, even toilet paper! Unemployment

---

[95] Revelation 19:7-9

is rampant, and people are being ordered to shelter at home and avoid human contact outside their homes. Businesses are in danger of going under, as malls and anything but those businesses deemed essential are closed. Even churches have been forced to close their doors when we need them the most!

Yet our God is finding creative ways to work good out of this crisis. Complying with the social distancing restrictions hasn't hurt our church at all. It's been shocking how many people were tuned in to our church's live-streamed services. And God's using many selfless people in these times.

A couple weeks ago on the front page of our local paper, the *Albany Democrat-Herald*, there appeared a stark contrast between the headline on the right proclaiming, "NYC virus death toll tops 9/11," and a photo parallel to it on the left with this caption: "Ryan Aman works from his garage to produce parts for medical face shields using his 3D printer. Aman, who works at Corvallis Clinic, supplies the shields to health care workers for free to help combat the coronavirus pandemic." [96]

With the shortage of critical supplies like shields and face masks, this man is using his own resources to supply free face shields to protect others. Also, the quilters in our town are making face masks, at their own expense, to fill the deficit. One quilter I know hasn't seen her husband in over a month because he's quarantined in a care facility that's gone to full lock-down, yet she's been working diligently to supply masks to the medical community. Our son Ben, a registered nurse, works in one of the hospital units most directly involved with caring for COVID-19 patients. The last conversation we had with him was through a screen door at a very great distance. He has taken many precautions to protect us, while putting himself at risk for others.

---

[96] *Albany Democrat-Herald,* Gazette Times, Publication number USPS 012-280, dated Wednesday, April 8,2020, (Lee Enterprises, Inc., entire contents Copyright 2019) Page A1, used with permission.

Conflicting and confusing predictions abound, and no one knows what life will look like even in the near future. But all is not lost. Amidst the craziness, turmoil, and heartache, there is a constant. Our Lord promised He'd be with us until the end of time, remember?[97]

In fact, even at the core of this pandemic, when concerns for the future are escalating, God is still finding ways to bring us joy.

In the early days of the COVID-19 pandemic, a mandate came through banning all large gatherings over 50 persons because of coronavirus containment protocols. My youngest son Stephen and his fiancée Anna were completely devastated! That meant their upcoming wedding they'd spent so much time orchestrating, agonizing over every detail, couldn't take place as planned on April 4, 2020. Nearly 180 of the invited guests had already responded in the affirmative, and that put them way over the maximum number now permitted for "small gatherings." After everyone cancelled their travel plans, Steve and Anna were too crushed to even formulate a new plan, the last time we'd spoken.

That's why on March 26, 2020, I was completely caught off guard by a call I got in Walmart, while I was standing right in the cold and flu aisle around all the hacking, masked people. It was my son Stephen, asking me if I'd gotten his text. No, hadn't heard it come through, I told him. He went on to tell me he'd sent a text asking for my blessing because he and Anna were "running off and getting married," as he put it. I thought he was joking; but when I found out he wasn't, I was totally elated for them! They'd found a willing minister to marry them in a scenic spot in Pennsylvania, and they were expecting to be at the destination in just minutes. I was whooping it up so loudly that one of the employees (whom I knew from church) came over to see what was going on! I was so happy for them that joy just

---

[97] Matthew 28:20

kept bubbling out of me all day long. I still had a smile on my face when I turned out the light to go to sleep that night, just praising God for transposing beauty for ashes, and pouring out the oil of joy in the midst of sadness.[98]:

Here's a photo of Steve & Anna, married March 26, 2020.

This current crisis will probably have lifted by the time this book goes to print, but either way we're still left with the question of the future, where we'll spend eternity.

Many times when I feared I'd blown it, I've taken solace in Jesus' words:

"Do not let your heart be troubled; believe in God, believe also in Me. In My Father's house are many dwelling places; if it were not so, I would have told you; for I go to prepare a place for you. If I go and prepare a place for you, I will come again and receive you to Myself, that where I am, there you may be also." (John 14:1-3)

---

[98] Isaiah 61:3

Do you know the way? Doubting Thomas didn't. Jesus hadn't yet died or been resurrected at this point, so the apostle Thomas said he didn't even know *where* Jesus was going, let alone the way."[99] That's when Jesus laid it out plainly, "I am the way, and the truth, and the life; no one comes to the Father but through Me."[100]

Are you still wandering in your own paths? Who are you following? If you're not yet fully following Jesus, the Shepherd of your soul, you've got to be following someone. Who do you follow on social media? Who are you putting yourself out there to impress? Whose opinions do you value?

Maybe you believe, "No one tells me what to do! I think for myself." But do you really? Do you even let yourself think about spiritual things that determine our eternal fate?

Someday we will all be held accountable for the decision we make, to follow Jesus, or to follow the world's standards and our own. Even in this world there are built-in consequences for rebellion and rejecting God.

"Be ready!" That was my brother-in-law Robert's famous line. But how many of you knew it was a quote straight from Jesus?

"For this reason you also must be ready; for the Son of Man [Jesus] is coming at an hour when you do not think *He will.*" (Matthew 24:44)

On July 3, 2012, my sister Kathy and her husband Robert celebrated their anniversary at Olive Garden with their grandson and my other sister and her husband. They all piled into the car afterward with Robert driving. Right in the middle of their hometown Robert suffered a massive, totally unexpected, heart attack. My other brother-in-law was barely able to wrestle

---

[99] John 14:5

[100] John 14:6

control of the wheel without all five of them being killed. How he finally got that car stopped I have no idea. It was horrendous. Robert died instantaneously, with no warning; but I am confident he was ready. It's not just because of his "Be ready" line he'd become known for, soberly warning others; but both my sisters and I saw a dramatic change in Robert. In the months leading up to his death, it was uncanny — it was like he was a different person. All three of us, without ever discussing it until after the fact, had detected a deep, spiritual transformation in him.

Are *you* ready?

Have you ever looked at the simple call Jesus made to His disciples? He beckoned to several of His would-be disciples on more than one occasion, saying, "Follow Me."[101] Some were commercial fishermen, and they just dropped their nets (their very lifeline) and followed Him. One was a tax collector named Matthew, who ended up writing the whole gospel of Matthew. Tax collectors were not viewed as exactly upstanding citizens. The people looked at them as thieves and traitors, taking the Jews' hard-earned money, pocketing some of it and/or cheating them, it seemed. And they worked for the tyrannical Roman government that usurped authority over the Jews of Jesus' time. Not popular folks! So what did Matthew the tax collector do when Jesus called, "Follow Me"?[102] He just got right up and followed Jesus! And there were many more who did likewise.

But not everyone was quite so ready to jump on the bandwagon. There was a rich young ruler who was curious as to what he'd have to do to get eternal life. He said he'd been following the commandments from his youth (not that anyone really can keep them all). But Jesus was God; He could read the man's heart and knew what was really tripping him up. Jesus challenged the man to sell all his possessions and give

[101] Matthew 4:19; Matthew 8:22; Matthew 9:9

[102] Matthew 9:9

them to the poor. Upon hearing this, the man went away grieving, "for he was one who owned much property."[103]

What holds you back? What obstacles are you allowing to bar your path to the Shepherd of your soul? What would it take to tear them down? How much do you want Him to turn up the heat to get your attention? He'll stop at nothing to see one of His lost sheep plucked out of the briars and put back on the path. But He chose to give us free will.

Who do you think put those barriers there? It wasn't God. God granted us free access to the Father through Jesus' own righteousness. He wants so badly to be known[104] by you, He made it simple:

If you "confess with your mouth Jesus *as* Lord, and believe in your heart that God raised Him from the dead, you will be saved; for with the heart a person believes, resulting in righteousness, and with the mouth he confesses, resulting in salvation."[105]

That's it! Too simple? Not intellectual enough for you? God is infinitely more complex than any human can fathom, but He allows Himself to be known. He makes it simple for us. Jesus said, "Truly I say to you, unless you are converted and become like children, you will not enter the kingdom of heaven."[106]

That summer in Dallas I described in the beginning, I spent some time in the Dallas County Jail. (*No, not as a prisoner, smile.)* A group of us from the college went to minister to the prisoners, and I learned something from one of those prisoners about the faith of a child. First the leader of our group preached from the beginning of the gospel of John: "In the beginning was

---

[103] Matthew 19:16-22; Luke 18:18-27

[104] John 10:14

[105] Romans 10:9-10

[106] Matthew 18:3

the Word, and the Word was with God, and the Word was God. He was in the beginning with God.... And the Word became flesh, and dwelt among us, and we saw His glory, glory as of the only begotten from the Father, full of grace and truth."[107] While he was preaching, one of the prisoners (an extremely good-looking guy, I inadvertently noticed) was prancing around his cell arrogantly, wearing only a towel.

Then our leader asked if any of us students would like to come up and share something with the men. I had no clue what I was going to say, but I stepped forward to the microphone. And I blurted out something like, "Probably some of you had a relationship with the Lord when you were children. I did too. Most young people seem to be drawn to Jesus first, but as a child I had a deep love for my Heavenly Father." I don't know what else I said, but I happened to glance in that towel-clad prisoner's face and saw tears in his eyes.

There is nothing quite like the faith of a child. And that's pretty much all God requires of us. Remember:

"And He [Jesus] called a child to Himself and set him before them, and said, "Truly I say to you, unless you are converted and become like children, you will not enter the kingdom of heaven. Whoever then humbles himself as this child, he is the greatest in the kingdom of heaven." (Matthew 18:2-4)

---

[107] John 1:1-2 and 14

"Striped Sheep"
(Courtesy of Audrianna Escobar, Age 5, pictured below.)

Epilogue

For Found & "Wanna-be-Found" Sheep: Fellowship

(Photo credit: Dave Schmidt)

In chapter five we were first introduced to the word fellowship, and I promised if you wanted to know more I'd put it in an optional epilogue. So here it is.

Okay, it's back to my old Webster's[108] for a specific definition of fellowship, because it's more of a "churchy" word, not used in other circles much because it actually doesn't exist in quite the same way there. I'll just list the first three definitions given, because the fourth and fifth don't apply here.

fellowship (fel'o ship') n. *[[ME felauship]]* 1 companionship; friendly association 2 a mutual sharing, as of experience, activity, interest, etc. 3 a group of people with the same interests; company; brotherhood[109]

The first definition is pretty basic, the kind of relationship I have with a neighbor who walked our neighborhood circle with me a week or so ago. We don't know each other well yet, but I'd like to be her friend. If it deepens, we could become regular companions, hanging out together, even becoming close friends. But that hasn't happened yet.

The next definition describes the second level of fellowship. It goes much deeper because you have something in common. How deep it goes depends on how deep the common ground is. If it's something like golf that brings you together, you might play golf together every six months if you're not an avid golfer. If you are a serious golfer, and the two of you play together often and share bits of your lives on the golf course, it may grow deeper gradually. But if the common interest you share is something that changed your life, it can penetrate much deeper.

---

[108] *Webster's New World College Dictionary*, Fourth Edition, Michael Agnes, Ed. (New York, New York: Macmillan USA, 1999)

[109] *Webster's New World College Dictionary,* Fourth Edition, Michael Agnes, Ed. (New York, New York: Macmillan USA, 1999), Pg. 521

Dave and I both lost a spouse. When we met online I responded to him just because he was a recent widower and I'd been widowed a long time by then. I wanted to help him through the hard spots. My daughter Sarah and her husband both lost their fathers when they were young. Alex was even younger than Sarah was when his dad died. That type of shared tragedy bonds people closer than cement, and quickly, if you open up.

But in the spiritual realm there's an even deeper, more profound, level of fellowship — on a personal level, which we'll start with — and on a group level like in definition three above, which we'll end with.

The very most personal fellowship of all is between us and God. When we say yes to following Him, and make Him Lord of our lives, it begins a journey that lasts a lifetime, as we get to know Him better and love Him more. I'm not going to treat that much here, because it's personal, between you and God. And everyone's relationship with the Lord is different. I'll let you and the Lord work that out.

But I will tell you a little about the kind of fellowship that occurs between believers on a one-to-one basis and how that has looked in my life and in the lives of others.

I've always been really close to my children, even when we were at our worst (trudging through their tumultuous teen years, practically locking horns). But when we share spiritually, one-on-one, our closeness goes even deeper. My sons and my daughter have different experiences, and different personalities; but we've all shared spiritually on some level. But fairly recently my daughter Sarah knocked my socks off by becoming a Christian, totally on her own, no help from me. And the fellowship, the depth of sharing we now have, is like nothing else in the world! We can share things people who've never given their hearts to Jesus couldn't possibly understand. Oh, maybe they could if they're somewhere on the road, actually.

I've seen that. And I'm not talking about an intellectual level of camaraderie, though that exists too when we do something like a Bible study together, but that's not it. It plunges so deep it goes to the very soul. We can tell one another things we wouldn't tell anyone else, and be understood without fear of mockery. Our husbands come first in the order of things and they always will (after God; everything's after Him), but when I share spiritually with any of my kids, the boys too, I feel that close fellowship that supersedes even the love I already had for them, and always will have.

Then there's that third definition of fellowship, the communal fellowship that comes with a group of individuals that have a common interest. When that occurs on a spiritual level, wow! It's hard to even explain.

On a more confined level it's found in a local church, especially in communal worship. But what I'm hoping to also describe to you is on a universal level, the communion of saints that's found in the entire body of Christ, across denominations, not confined to space or time, anywhere Jesus is truly lifted up. People who may not even know one another at all, but meet on a chance encounter or some planned function, have fellowship that can penetrate so far beyond the surface. It goes to the core of who we are, when we're Christians. It's hard to put into words. But if you know me at all, you know I'm going to try (smile).

Here's a true story I once wrote for a niece I care very much about who was getting ready to move to New York City. It describes the fellowship of believers. As you read it, notice my reaction when I find out the man is a Christian.

In the early 1970's I used to ride the subway from my home in the Maryland suburbs to my office in Washington, D.C. The daily commute was mostly uneventful, just a sea of faces blending together with no meaningful or life-altering interactions.

But that changed for me on one otherwise mundane workday commute.

At the time I'd taken to carrying with me a little, navy blue pocket New Testament. Reading helped fill the dead time on the train. I was a brand-new Christian then, so in awe of God's love pouring out of its pages that I could barely stand to put my Bible down.

On this particular day, immersed in reading my New Testament, I was surprised to hear a voice addressing me, asking if he could borrow my Bible. Taken aback, it took a couple seconds for his words to register. Verbal exchanges are pretty rare on the Metro. Looking up, I saw a rather nondescript older man addressing me. Just an ordinary commuter, I presumed. But once I realized what he was asking I was secretly exhilarated!

Someone actually wants to borrow my Bible! Maybe he's never even read it and this is my chance to bring him nearer to the Lord!

Without hesitation I handed it over, inwardly imagining what I'd say if he ever asked me a question. He held onto it a little longer than I'd expected, so I tried to act nonchalant, diverting my eyes from his face. Yet, excited as I was for this opportunity that had dropped in my lap, I knew the truth was that I was one of the shyest human beings God ever created. What would I say if he really did ask me a question?

A few minutes later he handed it back, saying he hoped I didn't mind that he'd written down a few things for me. Not knowing what to expect, I blurted out something like, "Sure, that's fine!"

Looking down, I saw he'd written several Scripture references, at least a couple of them from the book of Proverbs.

Like a dimmer switch suddenly turned up full blast, it dawned on me he wasn't some atheist in need of my feeble attempt to draw him to the Lord, but rather a bona fide believer.

My face was beaming with excitement that only a brand new and fully forgiven Christian can truly understand when I looked up at him and proclaimed, "You must be a Christian!"

He didn't utter a sound. Yet I still to this day — over 40 years later — can't adequately convey the look on his face when I made my bold assessment. It was a look of tenderness I've never before or since encountered, almost like a father looking at his newborn child for the first time. Even that doesn't quite describe it. I felt like I'd just looked into the face of God, or if that's too presumptuous, at least that of Billy Graham or an angel.

After thanking him, I gave my attention to looking up the Scriptures. Yet I couldn't fully concentrate on something that felt so important in a subway car crammed with strangers. I don't even remember seeing him get off the train while I was searching out the passages, and I never ran into him again.

I waited anxiously until I got home to delve into the Scriptures I'd been given. All the while it felt like I was carrying around a buried treasure just for me in my purse. Yet even when I settled into the privacy of my bedroom to read it I still couldn't fully understand all the passages written on the little folded paper.

The first Scripture was a soothing and uplifting look at God's love for us, His children. Very personal and very encouraging. Then there were several from the book of Proverbs about contention, one even about a contentious wife. Being single and in my 20's, just reading the word wife got my attention. I had no idea what the word "contentious" meant though. So I whipped out my old Webster's dictionary[110] and looked it up. *Ooh, this was not flattering!* It read, "contentious: always ready to argue; quarrelsome."[111]

Not what I was hoping to read at all!

And here's a sampling of the Scriptures about contentiousness that were sandwiched in between the beautiful and encouraging ones about God's intense love for us (for me even):

"It is better to live in a corner of a roof than in a house shared with a contentious woman." (Proverbs 21:9)

"... And the contentions of a wife are a constant dripping." (Proverbs 19:13)

I think, had this admonition been delivered by anyone else, I would have felt insulted. But it was delivered in such an indescribably loving manner, bound on either side by declarations of God's love, and it ignited a spark of hope for marriage. What's more, it was a secret only God knew about me, and one I couldn't possibly deny.

No human being had ever called me contentious, and pretty much only my family knew that side of me. As a child I was referred to by a teacher as, "sweet little Rosemary." That's the read most people got from me, and the only side strangers ever saw, with very rare exceptions. One exception was at my 16th birthday party. Contentious would have been way too mild a descriptive for the way I responded when I learned my parents were withholding my driver's license for a curfew violation.

---

[110] *Webster's New World College Dictionary*, Fourth Edition, Michael Agnes, Ed. (New York, New York: Macmillan USA, 1999)

[111] *Webster's New World College Dictionary*, Fourth Edition, Michael Agnes, Ed. (New York, New York: Macmillan USA, 1999), Pg. 314

God used that encounter with the stranger on the Metrorail in a profound way to shape me into the person I am today. And, in hindsight, I believe it also served as a warning for me, one that I later heeded. By the time God answered my prayers for a husband, He'd already been teaching me a lot from His Word about how precious in His eyes a gentle and quiet spirit is. That encounter on the subway was just the beginning of my preparation for marriage.

Was he an angel? I really don't know; but Webster's defines an angel as "a messenger from God."[112] In that loose sense, most assuredly he was.

The Lord continues to this day to amaze me, to correct me when I need it, and to shepherd me along His path.

And you never know when God's going to surprise *you*.

I don't want to get off on a tangent about angels from that story I just told you and take our eyes off the Lord.

That joy I felt as a new believer upon meeting someone and finding out he was a Christian was astonishing. At first you feel like a lone ranger until you discover there are plenty of others like yourself who share your experiences and your love for God. That fellowship with other Christians was such a joy once I adjusted to Bible college. We had great fun together and shared some deep things of God. I encountered unexpected fellowship in many other places too.

In Kentucky, for example, I happened upon a deaf man and every word of sign language I'd learned fled from my brain except three words, "Jesus loves you." At that, his face lit up in such a way that I knew for sure he was a believer and we connected on a whole new level.

---

[112] *Webster's New World College Dictionary*, Fourth Edition, Michael Agnes, Ed. (New York, New York: Macmillan USA, 1999), Pg. 53

At an international Christian conference in Ireland, the fellowship I experienced between people of a multitude of nations gathered there to worship together and proclaim Jesus was extraordinary! Praising Jesus out loud, each in our own language, with the songs and the teachings simultaneously interpreted in a number of languages, felt like a glimpse of heaven! This type of fellowship represents what is known as the communion of saints.

Remember, our fellowship as believers with God Himself is the highest level of fellowship. He already knows us intimately, but He wants to be known *by* us. It's almost like when Dave and I met on a Christian dating site and I had a picture on my bio but he didn't have one on his. It was a little frustrating, because I was really starting to like this guy after we'd made ourselves vulnerable, pouring out many details of our lives by email. Yet I'd never seen his face. It felt unfair, like he had a level of knowledge of me that I didn't have of him. I finally broke down and told him, and he didn't waste any time inserting a photo. But that reminds me of our relationship with God. At first He knows us so much better than we know Him. But as we give him our time, pray even the simplest, honest prayers, and read His Word, we get to know Him better and better and love Him more and more. It's hard to conceive how anyone could not.

A good, solid church where people worship the Lord and the gospel is preached is a great starting place for fellowship. The apostle Paul encourages us not to forsake this gathering together, saying, "let us consider how to stimulate one another to love and good deeds, not forsaking our own assembling together, as is the habit of some, but encouraging *one another*; and all the more as you see the day drawing near." (Hebrews 10:24-25)

Why is fellowship with other believers so important? Because in this world we and our "hard message" will be rejected by many. To walk the narrow path, we need support from others on the same road. There's joy in this fellowship that people who choose the other road will never experience in this world, nor, sadly, in the next.

As a reminder, here's a Scripture on fellowship from my sister, Kathy. She led me to the Lord, for which I am eternally grateful! And she and my other sister Jeanie have prayed for me all the way through this writing project (plus they're helping with editing):

"This is the message we have heard from Him and announce to you, that God is Light, and in Him there is no darkness at all. If we say that we have fellowship with Him and *yet* walk in the darkness, we lie and do not practice the truth; but if we walk in the Light as He Himself is in the Light, we have fellowship with one another, and the blood of Jesus His Son cleanses us from all sin."[113]

That fellowship includes welcoming the lost when they return. Here's a poem illustrating that inclusion of "lost and found" lambs in our fellowship. It's by Kathleen Ridgeway (my big sis), used with her permission. She based it on Isaiah 40:11:

---

[113] 1st Letter of John 1:5-7

"Little Lamb"

One of My tiniest lambs has been lost,
I must leave My flock and go find him;
He's very small,
No strength at all,
And darkness soon will fall.

One of My tiniest lambs has been lost,
I must leave My flock and go find him;
The wolves come out,
Are all about,
Will like him, there's no doubt.

One of My tiniest lambs has been lost,
I must leave My flock and go find him;
He's nothing to eat,
No warmth or heat,
Is that a little bleat?

One of My tiniest lambs has been found,
I must ask the flock to surround him;
We'll keep him warm,
And free from harm,
I'll hold him in My arm.

And when you've responded to the call of the Shepherd of your soul, what will He do with you? I guess it depends on what His purpose is for you in particular.

Let's see what Jesus had to say after He rose from the dead to Peter. Peter was a pretty mercurial character, if you see some of the stuff he did in the gospels, and then the change in him after Pentecost in the whole Book of Acts. He's the apostle who denied Jesus three times, finally cursing and swearing at those who accused him of being one of Jesus' followers. Let's look at Peter's conversation with Jesus:

"So when they had finished breakfast, Jesus said to Simon Peter, 'Simon, *son* of John, do you love Me more than these?' [The other disciples.] He said to Him, 'Yes, Lord; You know that I love You.' He said to him, 'Tend My lambs.' He said to him again a second time, 'Simon, *son* of John, do you love Me?' He said to Him, 'Yes, Lord; You know that I love You.' He said to him, 'Shepherd My sheep.' He said to him the third time, 'Simon, *son* of John, do you love Me?' Peter was grieved because He said to him the third time, 'Do you love Me?' And he said to Him, 'Lord, You know all things; You know that I love You.' Jesus said to him, 'Tend My sheep.' " (John 21:15-17)

What do you make of that? Did you notice the progression from tending little lambs, to shepherding the sheep, to tending the sheep? Cute, little lambs, starting out so innocent and pure, seem like they'd be quite the joy to tend. That's where Emily started out and got hooked. They then become somewhat older sheep, in need of actual shepherding and training. In the end they're fully-grown sheep, needing to be tended all the way to the end of the line.

We humans are pretty cute and soft when we're born too. Then we get a little older and need someone to keep us in line: a shepherd, such as a parent. Life flies by, and we're old sheep like I am now. Who knows how much tending I'll need toward the end of my life; I only hope I'm not too cantankerous.

But Jesus was addressing spiritual sheep, known as disciples, in His call to Peter. Jesus was commissioning Peter to carry on where He left off. After this discourse, and some personal information for Peter, Jesus repeated to Peter the same words He'd used to call him and his brother in the first place, "Follow Me."[114] The very first time Jesus is recorded as saying those words to Peter and his brother Andrew, he added a little something more, "Follow Me, and I will make you fishers of men."[115] Peter was a fisherman, after all, but I wonder if he fully understood in the beginning Jesus' prediction that he'd make him and his brother (who also became an apostle) "fishers of men." Which certainly is what happened, as you can see from the Acts of the Apostles and 1st and 2nd Peter, among other places.

But you may say, *I'm no Peter!* Well, neither am I. I've led a pretty quiet life. But the Great Commission, as the Scripture below has come to be called, is for all of us who follow Jesus:

"And Jesus came up and spoke to them, saying, 'All authority has been given to Me in heaven and on earth. Go therefore and make disciples of all the nations, baptizing them in the name of the Father and the Son and the Holy Spirit, teaching them to observe all that I commanded you; and lo, I am with you always, even to the end of the age.' "[116]

---

[114] John 21:19

[115] Matthew 4:19

[116] Matthew 28:18-20

The “nations” he sends you to might be found in a small town like the one I currently live in, or in a major metropolitan area or suburb. It could be a nursing home or a prison cell or another continent. Wherever you are and wherever the Shepherd of your soul leads in the future, safe journeys, my friends and family.

Love,

Rose

Made in the USA
Columbia, SC
25 May 2023

16911134R00062